The Yellowstone Wolves

the first year

The Yellowstone Wolves

Wolves

the first year

GARY FERGUSON

FALCON™

HELENA, MONTANA

10 9 8 7 6 5 4 3

Front cover photos by Alan and Sandy Carey.

Back cover photo of the Rose Creek pack, Yellowstone National Park, winter 1995-96, © Robert Winslow.

Design, typesetting, and other prepress work by Falcon Press, Helena, Montana.

ISBN 1-56044-500-9
Library of Congress Catalog Number 96-84578

Manufactured in the United States of America.

for number Ten

© Barry O'Neill

Acknowledgments

This book could never have been written without the life work and simple generosity of so many people. My sincere gratitude to Doug Smith, Mark Johnson, Mike Phillips, Steve Fritts, Bob Crabtree, Jim Peaco, Nathan Varley, Ed Bangs, John Varley, Joe Fontaine, Wayne Brewster, Bob Landis, M. A. Bellingham, Carrie Schaefer, Debra Guernsey, and Rick McIntyre, as well as to researcher Jan Falstad. And finally, a special thanks to biologists Rolf Peterson and Dave Mech, whose long years of dedicated research have given all of us such remarkable glimpses into the science and mystery of wolves.

Contents

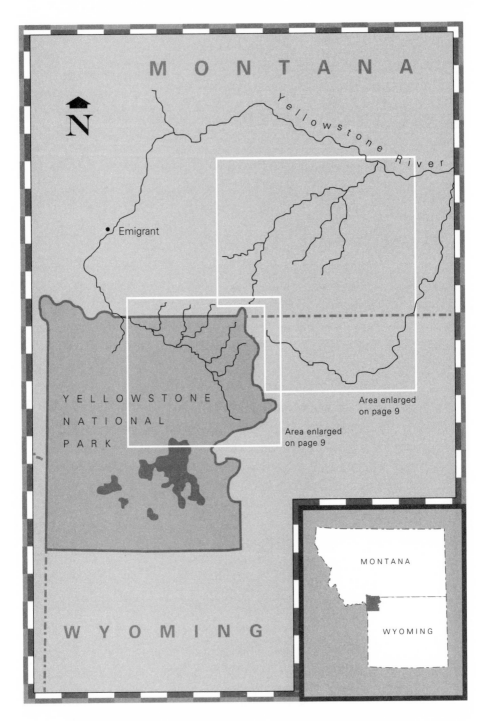

Yellowstone Country

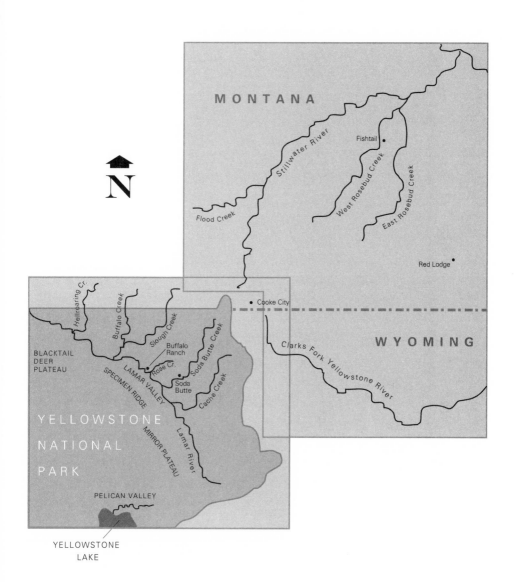

Wolf Country

Prologue

Beginning a journey with Yellowstone's wolves at the point they finally walk free in the wild is a leap of sorts, a tale without tracks. Starting as we do, in a snow-filled Lamar Valley in March of 1995, it's easy to forget the long years of sweat and hope that got us there in the first place. Sort of like a person taking her very first walk in the woods on a warm day soaked in spring, birds on the nest and flowers full in the meadows. It isn't a matter of not being able to grasp the magic of it; it's just that the magic seems even sweeter when you've known the depth of winter that came before.

Nearly twenty-five years have passed since members of Yellowstone's park staff, along with Assistant Secretary of the Interior Nathaniel Reed and a number of prominent biologists, came together in a meeting that would serve as one of the first steps toward wolf reintroduction in the nation's first national park. Yet another six years would pass before biologist John Weaver completed his exhaustive twelve-month survey of Yellowstone, looking for wolves by plane, on foot, and by ski, and finding none, finally recommending they be restored through reintroduction. And after that, long years of often bitter struggles, including more than a few meetings in the West that Hank Fischer has called "public wolf lynchings." More years still to nail down appropriations for an environmental impact statement—the blueprint for returning wolves to Yellowstone and northern Idaho—and two more, from 1992 to 1994, to complete it.

Even after all this, there was an extraordinary amount of work needed to actually get wolves to Yellowstone: Design and construct acclimation pens and transport containers, and work through a towering stack of permits and contracts and letters of agreement between

Canada and the United States; make certain that source wolf populations would come from areas free of rabies, tuberculosis, and brucellosis, and then develop a comprehensive disease sampling program; test out the net-gunning and other capture methods; set up security operations in Yellowstone to protect the wolves while they're in the pens. The list goes on and on.

And so as you travel through this first year with Yellowstone's wolves, know that every run of the Crystal pack up the Lamar, every howl from Soda Butte, every elk taken and pup born to Rose Creek, is but the bloom of seeds planted long, long, ago. So many times members of the wolf recovery team marveled to me about how lucky they'd been—how often things seemed to work out exactly right, in ways they never expected. Luck is a part of it, I suppose. But then again, maybe it's like the writer Cervantes said, that diligence serves as mother to good fortune. In which case I'd expect luck to be licking at the heels of Yellowstone's wolves for years to come.

The Yellowstone Wolves

the first year

ONE

It begins at a time of few beginnings. On one of those March days gray and sharp as steel, full of snow, winter still sprawling on its belly like some belligerent sow bear chasing the early bluebirds back down to the lowlands, showing no sign of ever giving Yellowstone back to spring. A time of illusions. Back and forward and back again, pulling and pushing, creatures of all kinds running after the season like beachcombers hurrying down the sand behind the surf hustling for treasures, only to be chased up the shore seconds later by the rush of waves. On the warm afternoons elk paw through to the ground for mouthfuls of fescue and wheatgrass, then lose their pickings the next day under a fresh layer of snow. Yesterday a mule deer carcass was starting to thaw under the drifts near Buffalo Creek, ripe enough with scent for any coyote within two hundred yards. By this afternoon it will be frozen fast again, barely detectable to even the best of noses. Tiny midges work their way up through layers of snow, food enough today for a couple of brave robins, by this evening out of reach.

Waiting. All of us, just waiting. For the glide of sandhill cranes. For the honk of Canada geese on the nest. And this year—the first time in almost seven decades—for the wander of wolves.

We're in that part of the park scientists have long considered a kind of wolf wonderland, lupis paradise—swales topped with dark coniferous forests; long, grassy meadows; and hushed, sheltered hollows rich with aspen. And best of all the Lamar Valley itself, winter home to great waves of wildlife—seven hundred bison and thousands of elk—and in late spring enough winter kill to fill the bellies of every kind of predator imaginable: coyote, raven, and mountain lion; grizzly and fox; eagle and badger and beetle. Three separate groups of wolves have been penned in this area since January—five animals near Soda Butte, six at Crystal Bench, and three at Rose Creek. And while at this point no one can guess where any of them will end up, after nine weeks of capture and confinement—surely about as close to nonexistence as a wild wolf could endure—life is about to start up again right here, an easy lope from the ice-laden waters of the Lamar.

The date is March 23rd. Two days since the gate was locked open on the Crystal Bench pen. After literally decades of preparatory research and logistical planning, after more public comments than have been received for any wildlife or environmental program in American history, after lawsuits and death threats and hate mail, the last barrier to wolves running free in Yellowstone has fallen. "We expected the wolves to dash out as soon as we stepped away from that gate," says wolf project biologist Doug Smith, a tall, lanky thirty-four year old fresh in from Minnesota. "In fact our biggest concern, what we planned for, was how best to get out of the way." Not that this concern was based on any sort of fear, mind you. More of a caution to give the animals the kind of space they'd need to leave feeling safe, calm, not prone to hit the great wide open at full tilt. An attempt to "soften" the release. And yet true to their reputation for unpredictability, to that uncanny habit wolves have of doing things that humans clearly don't expect and can't understand, getting out of the way is the last thing the recovery team needs to worry about. As it turns out there's plenty of time for the men to flip that gate open on the Crystal pen and hustle back to the trailhead without a single wolf leaving. Time enough down along the highway to grin and shake each other's hands, smoke a round of good cigars, sit at a pullout until two o'clock in the morning listening to the blip of the radio telemetry receiver, waiting to hear a change in direction. Getting nothing.

3

Six hours later the team is crammed back into mission control—the wolf office south of Mammoth, a tiny brown building fifteen by forty feet—scratching their heads. Maybe they're just afraid to leave, offers Doug Smith, pointing out the strong connections wolves might make between that open door and the humans who've been using it for the past ten weeks. Indeed, while there were few times when the men and women coming through that steel gate weren't laden with goodies, dragging frozen dinners of deer and elk and moose, in truth the wolves reacted to their presence with about as much enthusiasm as the rest of us might muster for a pot luck with serial killers. Pacing in the back of the pen in what would become known as their "comfort zone"—agitated, timorous, as if wanting to spit out the taste of the encounter. Seeing such behavior it's easy to believe stories from those who have long worked with wolves on Isle Royale, Michigan, who say that after forty years of living in that safe habitat, completely protected from harm, the vast majority of wolves still show every bit as much distrust of humans as their hunted kin in Alaska.

Park Service wolf project leader Mike Phillips, on the other hand, wonders whether even the concept of an opening may be a difficult notion for animals who've lived most of their lives without windows or doors, coming and going through the dark woods of

4

Alberta free of the need to pass into or out of anything at all. Of course no matter what the reason, there's a huge silver lining to the Crystal Bench's wolves' reluctance to leave the pen, a nugget of good news the team members can fondle whenever they start getting a little bummed over the fact that nothing's happening. It's simply this: At least they're not bolting for Canada.

Outside the scientific community theories about the wolves' hesitation are flowing like junk mail. Commentator Paul Harvey tells his listeners the wolves have become welfare wards, good-for-nothings, too fond of government handouts to ever want to go back and make an honest living in the wild. Never mind that early on many wore their teeth down and bloodied their faces from hours spent chewing on the chain link, trying to get out. Forget that to make any sort of bond with a wolf you have to be on it like a shadow almost from birth, feeding it from your own hand, sleeping with it every night, hugging it like a child with a stuffed bear. But then little of what is said concerning the Yellowstone wolves has much of anything to do with what's real. In the coming months these fourteen animals will rarely be cast as anything but gods or devils, the cure sure to save us or the plague that will bring us down—always either a team of saviors or a herd of Trojan Horses. Never just a bunch of predators, coming home.

The next day the team decides to leave the Crystal group alone and heads out instead to open the gate at Rose Creek. (An earlier thought, by the way, was to open the gate of each of the three pens seven days apart; that way each release could occur early in the week, when there were fewer visitors in the park. That idea was nixed, though, in part because some felt that dragging out the process over two weeks, with all the attendant media hype, might flame the anti-wolf people into an even bigger frenzy.) After opening the gate at Rose Creek the team returns to the Buffalo Ranch, sits in the

bunkhouse until well into the evening, pouring down hot choco-
late, playing spades and games of chess, waiting all over again. Once
more the monitoring equipment is silent. The only bright spot of   5
the day occurs later, up the valley, when the Soda Butte group (still
in their pen) lets loose with five minutes of the most exquisite howling imaginable—great licks of soul music, candy for the ears spilling
across the frozen landscape.

The next day Mike Phillips makes a call to noted wolf expert
Dave Mech back in Minnesota, who goes so far as to suggest these
wolves may well starve to death rather than walk into an area of the
pen that has such strong links to humans. If that's the case, reason
the team members, then what about providing them with a passage-
way in some other part of the pen, create an exit in a place to which
they have less aversion? The team is well aware of those so-called
comfort zones, the places along the pens with the long sidewalks of
packed ice from the constant pacing, the bowl-shaped depressions
nearby where the animals routinely bed down to rest. Perhaps all it
will take is to cut a hole in the fence right at the edge of that zone.
And so that afternoon a team heads to the Crystal Bench site and
cuts an opening ten feet wide and four feet high near the back of the
pen, then drops off a little incentive—two deer carcasses, placed
just outside the new exit. Bingo. Seventeen hours later, at 9:14 this
morning, a Crystal Bench wolf trips the monitoring equipment.
Then more signals. At 10:24, 10:27, 10:29, 10:30. Off and on for
the rest of the day. Wolves are out in Yellowstone.

*   *   *   *   *

Which takes us to the here and now—some three hours after
the Crystal wolves start walking out. Encouraged by that
success, a small team has arrived at the Buffalo Ranch, and is busy

stuffing fence cutters, a deer carcass, and an amazing array of camera equipment into backpacks, readying themselves to hike in and cut an opening in the Rose Creek pen. Project leader Mike Phillips is here, as is Doug Smith. There's wildlife veterinarian Mark Johnson, and photographers Jim Peaco, of the Park Service, and Barry O'Neill. And Ranger Bundy Phillips, one of the men responsible for maintaining the electronic monitoring devices in the area—Secret Squirrel equipment used not only for monitoring the movement of wolves through the pen openings, but also unauthorized human intrusions. As with most tasks when Mike Phillips is at the helm, this one has been laid out well ahead of time, precisely, matter-of-factly, sure to unfold like a S.W.A.T. team of surgeons. Everyone knows the mission: cut a hole in the back of the fence near the comfort zone to urge the male, female, and her yearling pup to leave; drop off a frozen deer carcass just outside that opening; set up a camera with a fixed focus in hopes of getting a shot or two of the wolves taking their big walk to freedom. And get out. The snow is falling harder— wet, heavy curtains snapped back and forth like sheets on a clothesline in heavy winds. To the south, dark lumps of bison amble along the river, appearing and disappearing, hulking animals looking strangely graceful, even spritely, tucked as they are into the curtains of the storm. The crew finishes loading the packs, dons snowshoes, walks off to the north into the face of the storm.

The three wolves waiting at the end of this long mush have, like most, endured a somewhat harrowing journey to end up in the United States, in this half-acre acclimation pen tucked into a wooded draw at Rose Creek. For the young pup, it began on a cold day in December of 1994, deep in the woods of Alberta, the thermometer having gone south, finally nodding off somewhere around minus thirty degrees. The wolves were being caught by Canadian trappers using a device known as a "modified snare," consisting of ten feet of fine steel cable suspended across a trail, with a loop at about head height that closes when an animal inadvertently sticks his head through it. The "modified" part is that instead of choking the animal to death, which is what happens to wolves that are captured for pelts, stops are inserted so that the snare wire closes around the neck only about as tightly as a typical dog collar. Some would later question why the somewhat more humane leghold traps weren't used to catch the wolves bound for Yellowstone and Idaho. But in the bitter cold of a January in Alberta, the trapped limb of any animal would have quickly frozen, leaving a gruesome legacy of three-legged wolves. It's interesting to note that, at the time these captures were going on, there were protests by a few Alberta residents over these wolves being taken out of the country, about Americans "decimating the population." It was an objection that struck some of the recovery team members as a little disingenuous. The fact is that the very wolves that ended up going to Idaho and Yellowstone would have been caught on those same trap lines, only the trappers wouldn't have been using modified snares.

Once caught, the animals were sedated by U.S. Fish and Wild-life biologists and veterinarians, who checked them for diseases and fit them with radio collars; these animals were then released again back to the wild to rejoin their packs. That done, the researchers went back home, returned again a month later, in January. This time, by following signals from the wolves captured earlier they were able to locate other members of the same pack—a clever, efficient way of going about things, but one that earned those first collared animals the somewhat unsavory name of "Judas wolves." The idea was that instead of taking a hodge-podge of individuals caught here and there and tossing them together at random—a method deemed okay for the Idaho wolves, since they'd be living in a much bigger slice of wild country—by using Judas wolves researchers could transplant members of the same pack. Families. And it was through the added measure of stability and comfort of families, scientists figured, that wolves would not only have less chance of getting on one another's nerves under the strain of being penned, but might also be more inclined to stay together, maybe even stay put, once the pens were opened. No one knew for sure if it would work, just as no one really knew much of anything else concerning how wolves would react to such incredible upheaval in their lives. No one, after all, had ever attempted to transplant them from the wild.

Snares used for catching live wolves are checked twice as often as killing snares—a lot of work, really, especially considering that most Canadian trappers have regular jobs elsewhere and trap on the side. On a typical winter day the whistle blows at the end of one job, the trapper climbs aboard his Polaris or Ski-Doo, and sets off for the outback to check his lines. It was nearly sundown on the 2nd of December when researchers received a phone call from one of those trappers working fifty miles east of Hinton, with two young sibling wolves caught in his snares. One turned out to be little number Seven—a bright, beautiful, reddish-gray pup now waiting in the Rose Creek pen. She was the youngest animal taken that season, and one that Mike Phillips will be smiling over for months, referring to her over and over again as "that dandy little wolf."

As per the plan, Seven and her sister were taken back to the research station, physically examined and radio-collared, then turned loose the next day. In January, Seven was caught again, this time helicopter-darted with her mother, who became Yellowstone wolf number Nine. Seven's sister, though, was no longer with them, having been shot and killed in the weeks between captures. And so it was that this mother and daughter—thought by then to be the only surviving members of their pack—would be among the first eight wolves to arrive in Yellowstone. Joining them in the pen after their arrival in the park was a lone wolf with no family at all, one that Nine and daughter Seven had never laid eyes on—a whopping, robust male that came to be known as number Ten. If there was one favorite wolf of all the workers in Canada, it was number Ten. The day he was caught this wolf weighed in at 135 pounds, which is extremely big for the wolves in that particular part of Canada. As it turned out he'd just fed, and much of that weight was in his belly; by the next day he'd slimmed down to 122 pounds—still a big wolf, matched only by the biggest animal of the Soda Butte group.

9

"Up in Canada I just started calling him 'the big guy,' " says veterinarian Mark Johnson. "He was different than any other wolf we had. When he was in that holding area, though never aggressive, he never broke his stare." Come transport day each wolf was drugged in order to ready them for the trip south. Typically workers would wave the handle of a snare pole in front of an animal's face, distracting it, making it easier to administer a shot to the hindquarters with a syringe fastened to the end of a long rod, called a "syringe pole." It always worked. "The more timid wolves even hid their faces in the straw through all of this," Johnson recalls. "But not number Ten. He held my gaze—never blinking, never looking away."

When Ten was first released into the Rose Creek pen with Nine and her yearling daughter, there was tension. "The big guy" snapped at Nine, drawing blood, generally sparing no effort to make it clear who was boss. All of which had the effect of leaving workers incredibly anxious as to whether or not their matchmaking efforts would in the end lead to a deadly match. They could only leave the wolves alone, give them time, wait it out. Then, just as quickly as the conflict started it seemed to evaporate. Things settled down. Tolerance caught breath, grew into a lasting peace. As the days passed the two adults first simply ignored each other, which was a tremendous improvement, then eventually began curling closer and closer together when it was time to rest.

10   The team members heading into Rose Creek today stop to catch their breath near a draw just east of the pen—the place where those faithful Park Service mules, Tack and Billy, usually stop when workers travel to this site by sleigh. From this location it's possible to see the southern-most portion of the half-acre pen, and today the men peer through the falling snow and see what looks to be the adult female, number Nine, trotting nervously back and forth, which is a little odd, because most times at the approach of humans Nine is hidden somewhere in her comfort zone at the back of the pen and it's Ten that's doing the pacing. The approach path drops into a small ravine hidden from the animals, then tops out again at the level of the pen. As a final precaution Mike Phillips will climb up and out of this ravine alone, peer over the lip of ground toward the pen to make certain the wolves are in fact still all there, at which point he'll wave the others on. As usual the talk is in whispers—not as part of some attempt to sneak up on the wolves; their noses alone, some hundred times more sensitive than ours, would make that all but impossible. The idea is simply for the team to throttle back the weight of its presence, to take some of the edge off the encounter.

And then it happens. "For a second or two I can't figure out what's going on," photographer Jim Peaco says about the long, soulful howl that erupts not ahead of him in the pen, where it should be, but from behind, on the open hillside to the east. One of the team members hurriedly retraces his steps back the way he came up the ravine and finds Ten standing on the ridge some ninety yards away, half-clouded in a curtain of snow, staring right at him. That confident stare. "His light gray color, the snow—he looked like a ghost," Jim Peaco says about first catching sight of him. "Just like a ghost." The howling goes on, spiced with a couple of curt barks, a hopping on his back legs, and a switching of the tail, classic signs of agitation.

The first few seconds are filled with something close to panic. Sinking, heart-in-the-throat distress. My God, Doug Smith is thinking to himself, eyes wide with alarm. What happens if our intrusion ends up pushing Ten out, sends him running across the wrinkles of Yellowstone without bothering to look back, prods him to head far afield when he otherwise wouldn't have, back north toward Canada, searching for signs of his old home? Has whatever social glue that's formed inside the pen gelled enough to hold a mother and yearling daughter together with a male who just nine weeks ago was a complete stranger? Or will this be the straw that breaks the family's back? Mark Johnson will later reflect on the questionnaire he sent out to captive wolf facilities around the country, asking what kind of behavioral reactions they should expect from putting wild wolves in pens and then letting them go. And how after having been of such great help answering every other question he'd ever posed to them—matters of pen design and feeding schedules and a long list of other things—on that fundamental question they were silent.

But Ten doesn't run. Apparently doesn't even consider it. The truth is that in some sixteen feedings from January through March this wolf was never inclined to recoil from humans in quite the same way the other animals did. Instead of pacing the far fence, hugging it like a prisoner on seeing the arrival of the hangman, Ten preferred to cruise at oblique angles to the workers, traveling along the less-beaten paths through the interior of the pen. Not showing aggression—none of the Yellowstone wolves offered the slightest hint of that. But not exactly cowering, either. Kind of like now. Phillips tells Mark Johnson and Doug Smith to drop the deer carcass, while Jim Peaco and Barry O'Neill fuss with setting up automatic camera gear in the midst of the chaos, fiddle for ten minutes with chilled, clumsy fingers, finally decide that it will take too long, give up on it, and begin to move out with the rest of the team. All the while Ten

12

stands on that hillside and continues to howl. In an effort to keep from making any movements toward Ten, the men hurry off by a different route, down the steep side of the ravine; at one point Barry O'Neill, carrying a camera lens the size of a small bazooka, slips off the icy slope and slides down the hill, wedging himself beneath a fallen tree. And still Ten howls. He begins trotting the ridge line to the east well behind them, following. The snow continues, big flakes now, here out of the wind falling plumb, as full of calm as that howl seems full of anguish.

For all the apprehension over the encounter, this is a brilliant, searing experience, a kind of time out of time. It leaves everyone buzzed and breathless, including one researcher who by his own admission has been studying wolves for so long that on some days the animals seem little more than bundles of potential behavior, creatures whose primary magic is their ability to throw wrinkles into the statistical norm. While team members are reluctant to guess the meaning of this or any other behavior, most find it hard not to think of such a display as entirely a reaction to their presence. A cry of intent. A bright, muscled howling of relationship and territory and propriety, from an animal who is clearly back in charge.

Well clear of the pen site, the men talk it out, over and over again. There's no doubt about it, Doug Smith keeps pointing out: Ten was upset. But while Phillips agrees, he says leaving was the last thing on that wolf's mind. In the final chilling, blustery minutes before their walking out at the Buffalo Ranch, some are reconsidering the old adages about the astonishing sociability of wolves, the desire to stick together that has staggered, confused, even horrified humans for centuries. "Man, think about it!" Mark Johnson says. "It'd be like escaping from prison and instead of high-tailing it out of there, which would be the sensible thing, you come back, wait and watch, try to break out your friends."

What no one can guess at this point—what no one would have dared even hope—is that this adult pair has moved well past the point of companionship. Despite being locked away in chain link, Nine and Ten have mated, and Nine is already swelling with pups. In just four more weeks she'll give birth to eight offspring in a makeshift scrape of dirt under a spruce tree high on a hill outside Red Lodge, Montana. Unlike most such births, though, she'll be alone when it happens—watching, waiting for her mate: big, bold number Ten. The animal who, for all his heart and bravado—a few might wonder if not because of it—will be the first of the Yellowstone wolves to die.

*   *   *   *   *

Rose Creek's number Seven—Phillips' "dandy little wolf," the yearling from Alberta who arrived with her mother—begins showing a strong independent streak not long after walking out of confinement. She's a part of the group and yet apart from it, joining her mother and Ten on their rambles north of the park along Buffalo Creek and later near Sheepherder Peak, but spending time poking around on her own, too, often even bedding down at night well away from the adults. In time she'll begin making more and more forays on her own, heading back to upper Rose Creek above the old pen site, the following week drifting west into what will become one of her favorite haunts, the shadowy twists of Hellroaring Creek, where early on she'll make her first known kill of an elk calf. Meanwhile mom and her new partner are for a time content to hang out with the moose north of the park at Bull Creek, near Frenchy's Meadows—that splendid sweep of open grassland cradled by vast runs of timber, most of it torched by the 1988 fires. Thousands of acres of burn, black and blonde against the drifts of spring snow.

After being seen on April 13th in that same general area, this time again with the wandering yearling, Nine and Ten pack it in and move. A tracking flight on April 18th spots Seven, nearly to Tower Junction, but Nine and Ten are nowhere to be found. Another flight on the 19th, and again on the 20th, and still another on the 22nd turn up nothing. The two have disappeared like birds in the night on the run from winter, vanished from their haunts among the patchwork of forests at the park's northern tier, from the flats of Frenchy's Meadows, magicians blinking off the stage in a puff of smoke. It's not until eleven days later, on April 24th, that biologists finally find them again, some forty miles away, past a cast of high country as rugged and imposing as any in Montana, on the piney flank of the very last mountain on the way to the Great Plains.

TWO

The Soda Butte wolves don't spend a lot of time sitting around thinking about getting out. True, for almost two-and-a-half hours after researchers cut a gaping, eight-by ten-foot hole in the fence near their comfort zone and drop deer carcasses just outside, the group alternates between rounding the pen, giving the hole a wide berth on every lap, and just sitting fifteen or twenty feet away from the cut, heads cocked, staring out. But in the last light of evening a couple of the bolder animals decide to chance it—make their way through the opening, move ten feet or so beyond it to grab a carcass, pull it back into the pen, and begin to feed. Three groups of Yellowstone wolves, and three very different styles of getting out. It's worth noting that the first steps back into the wild for this group are on ground not far from where the last Yellowstone wolves were wiped out sixty-nine years before; two frightened pups just west of here, caught in leghold traps and killed.

By the following morning the Soda Butte group is out for real, all five of them, wandering around casually, managing to kill an elk calf about a half-mile from the pen. This quick take leaves some thinking that while three months of delays due to lawsuits may have

16

added tens of thousands of dollars to the expense of this program, as far as the wolves are concerned the later release might have been a good thing. It's now, after all, late winter, when wildlife are most vulnerable. And as far as these wolves are concerned, it's prey vulnerability, not numbers, that matters most.

Running with the bunch today is wolf number Thirteen, long known to some as Blue, a handsome male that filmmaker Bob Landis refers to as the Gray Ghost—in part because of his color, but more for his coyness, his tendency to stay in the background whenever humans come cruising up and down the Lamar Valley, gawking and taking photos. Based on the wear of his teeth and the stained color of the enamel—a color the Canadian trappers in Hinton say they haven't seen in decades of trapping—the Gray Ghost is thought to be the oldest animal brought to Yellowstone. Though actually a gray wolf, the blue cast is a fairly rare genetic trait, on top of which is the sophisticated-looking silver coloring that sometimes creeps over certain wolves, dogs, and of course humans as they age. In the acclimation pen Ghost was best known for making mad dashes into one of the dog house-style security boxes every time the recovery team approached. That habit's especially interesting when you consider that, other than a few animals who used the roofs of these structures as watchtowers, the security boxes were more or less ignored by every other wolf in Yellowstone. One day Ghost must have been asleep at the switch or maybe daydreaming of better times, because several humans entered and caught him out on the other side of the pen, far from his box. On realizing his mistake the poor fellow panicked and made a headlong dash for the box, running for the hole like someone was shooting at him, all but brushing against a surprised volunteer standing nearby with a frozen leg of elk in her hands, diving in through the opening of the heavy box so hard he slammed against the back wall and actually tipped it, not to venture out again. So much for big bad wolves. It's the Ghost Bob Landis catches on film on this first morning of freedom, the old boy running like a teenager through the open country along the Soda Butte drainage.

As the days go by the Ghost's personality will change completely from the one researchers came to know in the acclimation pen. Feeding in the wild he'll often be spotted high up in the chow line, eating from a position clearly reserved for higher-ranking wolves. What's more, his howling appears to be important to the rest of the pack, bringing the others running as if he were some wise master calling his students at the start of zazen; an image spun out of those old tales from the Orient about the blue wolf, the thunderbolt, thought to be the manifestation of heaven's light. It will be nine months before researchers figure out that Blue is in fact the alpha male of his group.

Also part of the team is a big, dark two- to three-year-old male the color of good earth—one with a strange injury to his left foot, leaving it splayed out, Charlie Chaplin-style. Number Twelve. When seen from a distance running across the snowy hills—and splayed foot notwithstanding, this wolf can run—you might at first think somebody's black lab had broken leash and was off to the outback, determined to turn himself into something wild. It's Splayfoot, who appears younger and more dominant-acting than the Ghost, that biologists consider the most likely candidate for alpha male. As to just how old either Splayfoot or the Ghost really are it's hard to say. Aging live wolves is a surprisingly inexact business, based almost entirely on the wear and staining of teeth. Females can be slightly easier, thanks to clues in their reproductive structures. After a female breeds her teats will be larger and darker colored than they were before; finding a wolf with those characteristics, then, at least you can confirm that the wolf is in fact a breeding adult. The remainder of the Soda Butte group consists of two mottled grays—which look like nothing so much as big coyotes with very long legs—and one small black yearling male, number Fifteen.

It's a bit of a wonder that Fifteen is even around for these first steps through Yellowstone. He was one of the animals darted during the initial capture effort in Canada, one of those so-called Judas wolves, collared and released to lead recovery team members to the rest of his pack. In truth Fifteen was a lot more subordinate than most of the wolves seen that winter—cowering, uncertain of himself, not exactly the kind of breeding stock scientists might pick if they had a choice. When he was recaptured in January, though, something was clearly wrong. The tranquilizing agents were having a serious, alarming effect on him, sending him into a far deeper anesthetic state than anyone would have expected from the dose he received. Concerned, Dr. Terry Kreeger reached for the portable pulse oximeter, a high-tech piece of medical equipment used to measure the amount of oxygen in the blood by passing a light beam through the tongue. In a healthy wolf the reading would be around 97 or 98 percent oxygen. Little Fifteen, though, came in with a shocking 55.

Unknown to anyone, when Fifteen was first helicopter darted, the tranquilizer dart drove past his rib cage all the way into his body, allowing a positive pressure to form against his lung, collapsing it. Using an ambulatory bag designed for humans, Dr. Kreeger manually ventilated Fifteen for forty-five long minutes, pushing the lung out against the cavity while another veterinarian, Dr. Janet Jones, sewed up the wound. Two days after the operation, when Fifteen was drugged and processed for transport, the pulse oximeter read 75. Not exactly recovered, but better. The last hurdle was for him to avoid complications, most notably pneumonia, which he managed to do just fine, living on to thrive first in the acclimation pen, and now on this special day of coming out, running through the grass and lingering patches of snow near Soda Butte, stopping now and then to fill himself with the smells of his new home.

Biologists predicted some time ago that if any group was likely to say adios to each other on release and run off to the hinterlands, it was this one. The Soda Butte wolves were never what you could call a classic family—just a young rag-tag crew of related animals apparently without the leadership of their alpha male and female wolves. And it's the alpha pair that serves as the core, the building block of a wolf pack. Yet so far no one seems the least bit inclined to strike out as a lone wolf. During the first weeks out, this group will hang together, staying closer to the pen than either of the other two groups, loping up and down the Soda Butte drainage, bringing down a handful of elk early on, a royal family content to roam the grounds, take stock of its new estate. Eastward to Cooke City one day, just as quickly back again. Up Amphitheater Creek, then a return. Possibly to Cache Creek, a U-turn, and back. In contrast, the Crystal and Rose Creek groups seem to be handling the business of finding territory by making forays outward, toward the edge of some vague perimeter we know little about, then backing up—like shipwrecked survivors on some island trying to get a sense of things by walking the shoreline. By mid-April the Crystal group will have run east out of the park all the way to Red Lodge, as will the two adults of the three Rose Creek wolves.

The Soda Butte group, though, maneuvers more from the inside out, castaways preferring to run small circles of discovery from the point where the ship first ran aground. Even though they were the last to be set free, in the early weeks wolf watchers along the roadway stand as good if not a better chance of seeing these animals than those of any other group.

While in the warm months wolves prefer to travel during the cool of evening and night, in winter they can be active virtually any hour of the day. And in Yellowstone, March still holds a lot of winter. Some research suggests that heavy, pouring rain may serve to dampen wolf wanderlust a bit, and thirty or forty below zero with the wind running at full tilt may push them to hunker down in heavy cover for a time, but for the most part what we would consider nasty weather—anything but heat, that is—doesn't faze them at all. Wolves do make concessions to heavy snows, opting to travel on roads, wind-scoured ridges, game trails, or even frozen waterways, though they're not fond of bare ice. If the layer of fresh snow is deep and powdery, the animals will follow each other in a line, the trailing wolves sometimes placing their paws so precisely in the footprints of the lead animal that even to experienced field biologists it can at first look like a single track. In the worst snows they often move forward not by walking so much as jumping ahead and resting, like somebody trying to cross a river by leaping onto one boulder, pausing, then leaping onto the next.

While the business of checking out new territory in and around Yellowstone requires lots of travel over uncertain ground, the Soda Butte wolves, like the other groups, are establishing trails that will be used over and over again in the weeks to come. In subsequent years some of these routes will become part of extensive trail circuits, some perhaps forty or more miles in length, entrenched wolf highways that in places will link to pathways used by adjacent packs. During these forays into new country, the wolves are also marking with scent, just as an explorer might place flags on newly discovered lands. These scent marks serve as correspondence for pack members as well as for other wolves—even for other species, like coyotes.

Around mid-April the Soda Butte group begins moving through the snow-filled lodgepole forests northeast of the park, out into the rugged mountainscapes of the Absaroka-Beartooth Wilderness. Heading out of the deep woods they soon arrive at the dramatic, wind-blasted Lake Abundance Basin, then push on for another fifteen miles down the Stillwater Valley—an astonishing wonderland of soaring rock walls hung with waterfalls and mountain goats and long reaches of burned timber. What makes them go? Why now? How incredibly strange it must be for these animals, whose movements are typically influenced to a great degree by sight or scent of other wolf packs, to most days be able to strike off in three out of four directions without finding hide nor hair of their own kind. In the life of a free-ranging wolf, that's likely about as weird as it gets.

This trek to the Stillwater is hardly a final farewell to Yellowstone; a couple weeks later the Soda Butte group ventures a return, using more or less the same route. On a blustery day in early May, a handful of Yellowstone elk begins moving briskly down a hill just north of the Lamar Valley highway, near the rock formation called Soda Butte. It's exactly the kind of movement wildlife watchers look for, a first hint that predators may be in the area. Sure enough, a couple of minutes later an adult grizzly comes ambling along through the trees heading the same direction—not really pursuing the elk. Just keeping in touch. In time the elk and then finally the bear vanish from sight into the woods; curiously, a few seconds later another small herd—this one several hundred yards away—begins trotting down the slope in the opposite direction. This time, though, it's no bruin sniffing at their heels, but three members of the Soda Butte wolves, including that easy-loping, black labish-looking Splay-foot. The group lies down on the side of the hill for a few minutes, resting and watching the elk, taking in the action like fans in the bleacher seats of a football game. Then, as if somebody fired a starting gun, all three leap to their feet in the same instant and spring off in pursuit of the bear, at which point the young bear turns his stubby tail around and makes for the hills.

22

The next day the Soda Butte group heads still further south, to that exquisite sprawl of meadow and spruce south of the confluence of the Lamar River and Soda Butte Creek. The crossing of this river seems especially significant, because in a lot of places such major waterways serve as territorial boundaries, just as the Lamar has long been a kind of property fence for the valley's coyotes. In fact with this crossing the Soda Butte wolves do indeed find themselves smack in the middle of a heavily traveled wolf-way used by the Crystal pack in their comings and goings to and from Cache Creek, further upstream along the Lamar. That fact doesn't escape them. Suddenly the Soda Butte animals are getting great snootfuls of scent laid down over the past month by other wolves, which apparently leaves them with a certain longing for their own quiet, unsullied digs far to the northeast; shortly after their arrival they make a U-turn, swim back across the Lamar River, and head for their Stillwater home.

As it turns out, not every member of the Soda Butte pack is along on this little expedition. One wolf, a young, gray female known as number Fourteen, missed out on the outing altogether, choosing instead to stay behind on the Stillwater. The truth is Fourteen is pregnant—perhaps has already given birth. Along with Rose Creek's number Nine she's the second female to have mated in the pen, this in a year when no one was supposed to be in the mood for mating. Right now she's waiting above the Stillwater, far from her acclimation pen, in a jumble of boulders near a rugged, choppy drainage in the northeast corner of the Beartooth Mountains called Flood Creek.

With some million acres in this ecosystem to choose from, Flood Creek seems an interesting choice for a wolf home. It's very different from the lands found along Slough or Buffalo or Bull creeks, or any of a number of other meadow-forest complexes these wolves have tramped through on their way to and from the Lamar. Clearly there's no shortage of prey here—deer and elk and moose—though in sheer numbers they're nowhere near as plentiful as they are closer to Yellowstone. Nearly all the timber here was burned to a crisp in 1988, in that astonishing bit of undoing known as the Storm Creek Fire. This particular drainage was more thoroughly burned than most; after seven years and a recent wave of blowdowns the surrounding heights are shocking in their austerity—bald spines and splinters of rock, mountains without flesh. Not so, though, when it comes to the bottomlands. There the shock comes not from the lack of plant life but the overwhelming abundance of it. The snow is melting off to reveal six-inch-thick mats of grass, as well as nearly impenetrable thickets of young chokecherry and currant, rose and aspen and lodgepole, the latter growing about two feet high and eight to ten to the square yard, spring-green and bristled, looking from a distance like a field of bottlebrushes. Such thick plant growth would make it nearly impossible for wildlife to avoid ambush; indeed, in most places here you could be standing within five feet of a crouching predator and never know it. And yet in truth that may not matter much to the Soda Butte wolves. Unlike their kin in the far north, or like mountain lions and bobcats, these wolves probably aren't much into ambush-style hunting. Given half a chance they'll run an elk or moose or deer—searching for a limp or other weakness or seeking advantages like deep snow—then finally overpower the animal.

On average an alpha female wolf will give birth in late April or early May to a litter of six pups. The Rose Creek female, number Nine, will beat that average by a third, having eight. But Fourteen's experience is much different. Despite great efforts by researchers in the weeks following her apparent whelp to confirm the presence of little ones during routine tracking flights, from all appearances it seems the Soda Butte group has grown not by six, not even four, but by just one. One little pup trailing the pack, as spotters will note from the air, stumbling across a meadow on short, uncertain legs, doing his best to keep up with the adults. No one will ever know whether that one pup is all there ever was (which is certainly not unheard of), or if in fact more whelped and then were lost. It's conceivable, though not necessarily likely, that the stress of confinement may have compromised Fourteen's health or fertility, resulting in just one pup being born. Also, around the time this pup was born, researchers noted most members of this pack traveling about hunting, often leaving only Fourteen and Fifteen near the den. Given the rugged terrain here it may have been fairly easy for a hungry mountain lion to come out of nowhere and make a quick meal of a wolf pup or two. While on the whole wolves seem to be consistently better mothers than domestic dogs, this was Fourteen's first time giving birth. Could her lack of experience have led her to choose a less than ideal den site?

For roughly the first two weeks Soda Butte's junior wolf will be blind and deaf, life consisting mainly of nursing (drinking a good eight ounces of milk at just ten or eleven days old), and either whining for attention or crawling around looking for it. After about two weeks his eyes will open, though his vision will be poor, and when not sacked out he'll be standing, growling, even walking and chewing. At three weeks his ears will start working, and he'll get to go outside the den and cavort a bit. (Assuming, that is, that mom had time to adequately prepare for all this, and there is in fact an actual den to go out of.) Three weeks, around mid- to late May, also marks the time when he'll stop dining only at Mom's place. From then on he can also merely touch the mouth of any adult in the group— mother, father, step-siblings—to stimulate the older animal into regurgitating meat. While the early weeks of Junior's life are a lot about eating, sleeping, and staying warm, there are also social ties being formed, ties that will help anchor the strong sense of relationship that ultimately allows a group of wolves to stay together and prosper in relative peace.

Speaking of staying together, the focus required to caretake young animals like this one is one of the things that helps build cohesiveness among members of a wolf pack. Which again is why even though biologists didn't expect breeding activity to occur this year, they still put a lot of effort into trying to bring family groups to Yellowstone. There's never been any attempt to keep wolves inside the park; no biologist in his or her right mind has ever suggested something so preposterous. Nonetheless, packs that face the task of raising young don't have the option of roving about the countryside in quite the same way pupless wolves do, at least not until fall, when the kids are finally able to travel. That kind of careful selection of which wolves would come to Yellowstone, along with soft release methods, will pay off handsomely in the coming months. When naturalist Jim Halfpenny begins generating maps highlighting the movements of both Idaho and Yellowstone wolves, it'll become very obvious that the Yellowstone animals are on the whole a much tighter, less ranging group. Indeed, had Yellowstone's wolves ranged as far and in the same direction as those in Idaho, most of them would be somewhere north of the Yellowstone River and Interstate 90, smack in the heart of ranching country.

Had the Soda Butte pup been blessed with surviving siblings his social studies would have been even more complete—first from three weeks spent nestled together in the den, and later through a variety of ritual play. On the other hand, while Soda Junior may lose out on the play thing, maybe there's something to be said for the amount of attention he'll get as an only child. Wolves are famous for being attentive to pups; just think how spoiled you could get with five adults fussing over you.

It's hard to imagine being born in a year with this particular slice of the world more filled with life. Thanks to an abundance of late-season moisture the bracken fern around Flood Creek is unfurling with abandon, soon to grow into chest-high plants— dinosaur gardens—and the air will be heavy with the scent of wild rose. As the weeks pass, streams that have not run for years will flow bank to bank, lasting much of the summer, while the Stillwater will be anything but, running wild and crazy, leaping off the rocks in great white sprays through much of June, as if it were trying to jump back to the sky. Snakes and mice are thriving in weaves of grass, which in turn are attracting an abundance of hawks, now soaring high above the river, now perched in the skeletons of burned trees.

A short lope from this pup's birth site, beyond the foot of Cathedral Peak, the land is exploding with wildflowers: phacelia and stonecrop; leopard lily, forget-me-not, clematis, and geraniums; strawberry, harebell, umbrella plant, and bluebell; pasqueflower and arnica—and in the open meadows lupine, waist-high and blue as the deep sea, mixed with the bright gold, nearly electric blush of balsamroot. Butterflies—mourning cloaks and red admirals—as well as calliope hummingbirds, are already beginning to dance. Moose saunter past well below the den site, as does the occasional bull elk, his new rack of antlers still wrapped in velvet, and spreading fast. The time is coming for a curious pup to poke and prod at this grand whirl of life, to run and sniff and roll until he drops in a heap of sleep.

*   *   *   *   *

The Slough Creek valley, which lies both in and beyond the northern reaches of the park, is becoming a major corridor of travel for the Soda Butte group. This is a stunning place in every season; on warm days in late May and early June, when the grass is Kelly green and long parades of cumulous clouds come rolling off the Buffalo Plateau, it can almost break your heart. Here, in the third week of May, there are yet a few lavender pasqueflower blooms huddled around tufts of sage, as well as bright yellow splashes of buttercup. Mergansers and Canada geese are in the quiet backwaters, and red-tailed hawks are on the nest. In the last of the twilight sandhill cranes continue to toss their wild, laughing songs across Second Meadow, where moose are pitched forward on their knees, better to nip at the green shoots of flowering plants. Coyotes, both singly and in small groups, move at quick trots up and down the valley on both sides of the Creek. As is often the case these days, in some of the muddy stretches of trail I find fresh tracks from the Soda Butte wolves.

The week after my latest visit, on a warm, sun-drenched Memorial Day, wolf project veterinarian Mark Johnson and his partner Nancy Loren, along with friends Robin and Theron Miller from Missoula, are heading out of the upper Slough Creek country after three days of backpacking. Around ten o'clock they call a break, settling in on a ridge overlooking the long runs of meadow that cradle the east and west sides of the waterway. As usual they waste no time pulling binoculars out of the packs and glassing the valley; these last few days have already offered some choice elk watching— a loose toss of cows grazing along the bottoms, many with calves nearby, all but invisible nestled in the tall grass and behind olive-colored clumps of sage.

When Robin first glimpses two black heads poking above a small rise some eight hundred yards away, they don't register with her as being wolves. As far back as anyone can remember spotting a black-headed predator in Yellowstone could only mean one thing: bears. But when the animals come to the rise and begin walking in the direction of the watchers, it's clear that these are not bears at all. Having worked closely with virtually every wolf that ended up in either Idaho or Yellowstone, it doesn't take Mark Johnson long to identify the pair: one is number Twelve, Splayfoot, and the other is Fifteen, the small male who nearly died in Canada from a collapsed lung. The wolves are progressing eastward by turns, one lying down and watching while the other walks slowly forward, and then switching roles, all the while creating a zig-zag track across the meadows. A search pattern. When the cow elk standing on the far side of Slough Creek notices their approach she grows agitated, out of sorts. She begins barking. But still they come.

Then in what seems like the most casual of movements Twelve walks to his left about six feet, grabs hold of the head of an elk calf that's been lying hidden in the grass, drags it ten feet or so across the ground, then holding his bite, simply lies motionless over it. There's no shaking of the calf, no sense of ferocity in the attack. The cow elk, though, goes berserk, begins chasing number Fifteen, who seems to be intentionally leading her in wide circles away from the calf. "A few years back," Mark Johnson recalls, "I saw a cow elk chase coyotes away from a hidden calf. That was a confident, determined kind of chase, as if there was no question about who had the upper hand. But this encounter with wolves is different. The cow's more careful. Sometimes she backs off from Fifteen as if sensing she's too close, waits a few seconds. Then re-launches the pursuit."

For some twenty minutes the cow elk continues to chase Fifteen, during which time four coyotes, curious about the commotion, enter the scene at a run; when they spot the wolves they stop, holding back at a distance of about a hundred yards. One of the coyotes raises up on his hind legs, begins hopping up and down, barking loudly at the wolves. Coyotes, of course, are also hardly a welcome sight to an elk with calves, and on sighting them the cow grows even more upset. She gives up the chase on Fifteen and goes after the coyotes instead, gets right on their heels, sends them scrambling off across the meadows. Meanwhile Twelve gets up from the calf, walks over to Fifteen, and the two then lie on the stream bank, watching. A pair of Canada geese drop out of the blue and settle onto the cool, slack waters of Slough Creek, immediately opposite the wolves.

The coyotes are off in the distance, regrouping, discussing their options, right where Robin first spotted the wolves; one urinates and then rolls in the exact spot where wolves Twelve and Fifteen had been standing a short time before. When the elk calf raises its head Twelve gets up from where he's been lying, strolls back over, grabs hold of the calf's muzzle and again lies there motionless. After this the prey never moves again. The cow elk, sensing she's lost her calf, finally moves off, and Fifteen, after a lengthy period, goes over and begins feeding on the carcass—calmly, without making any overt claims of social rank, both expending only as much energy as they need to, the heat of the day pushing them, now and then, belly deep into the waters of Slough Creek. On a couple occasions Fifteen drags the carcass, snagging it against the sagebrush, as if maneuvering it to better allow him to tear pieces of the meat.

By this point some two hours have passed since first spotting the wolves; other hikers have come along and joined Mark, Nancy, Theron, and Robin. Unfortunately some of the new watchers aren't savvy to the effect of sudden movements, of loud voices, and at one point Twelve and Fifteen suddenly look over and see the people, turn and trot quickly away toward the coyotes, looking over their shoulders as they depart. At their approach one of the coyotes raises his leg and urinates—an indication of his alpha status—and then in a fit of outrage begins chasing the wolves up the hill, at times coming within ten feet of them. This is denning time for coyotes, and there may well be pups nearby. Twelve turns once or twice and chases the alpha coyote back, but his heart just doesn't seem to be in it. Maybe it's just too hot for chasing. The last anyone sees of the wolves is as they disappear into the lodgepole forest on the far side of the creek, the alpha coyote still in pursuit.

The death of the elk calf is already serving other life. Ravens are never more than a half-step behind wolves, and sure enough one settles on this carcass almost before Twelve and Fifteen are out of sight. A minute or two later a bald eagle comes along, and he too begins to feed.

THREE

Number Ten's last look at the world comes midmorning on a warm Saturday in April, from atop a sage-covered hill outside the old coal mining town of Bearcreek, Montana. Edge country, where the mountains and the high desert come hip to hip, cradling a patchwork of croplands that spill across the bottoms toward the Clarks Fork River. A place of magpies and mule deer, of big spring winds and soil that puddles to grease in the wake of melting snow. The ground Ten is wandering over yields sweeping views—south toward the oil patch country of northern Wyoming, east to where the sun hovers above the tilted plateaus of the Pryor Mountains, some forty miles away. While it's true there's no shortage of mule deer in these draws and coulees, not to mention elk roaming the pine and aspen woods to the south, it's probably safe to say that this is the extreme edge of what most wolves would consider good home turf. Downslope the lands are increasingly dappled with ranch houses and small towns, the ground parceled by barbed wire. Country worth exploring, maybe. But not settling.

To say that some of the people living in those ranch houses and small towns aren't overly fond of wolves is sort of like saying some Baptists don't seem overly fond of the devil. A few are more than willing to give wolves powers of evil that would make Stephen King cringe with embarrassment, stuffing wolves with a depth of gloom and viciousness that strikes those who don't live in the rural West—as well as a great many of us who do—as utterly inexplicable. Against that background it's easy to assume that the man on the road above Scotch Coulee this morning pulling a borrowed 9mm rifle out of the back of his pickup, leaning in against the cab and setting an uphill aim over some one hundred and forty yards, pulling the trigger, killing number Ten with a single shot, is acting with clear intent to rid this country of wolves. And in a strange way, casting it like that, as the work of a zealot, might somehow make it easier to take. Easier than a killing that's little more than a thoughtless act, a bit of brazen swashbuckling fueled by a few beers and a little ganga, the latest in a long line of firing guns at coyotes and dogs and God knows what else—often intending to kill, but on occasion shooting with the intent of scaring, of coming close. "I can't believe it," Chad McKittrick will tell me later in a rare moment of shell shock, sharing what, if true, would bring new meaning to the notion of wandering around with a black cloud over your head. "I just can't believe I actually hit it. Shit, I've been shooting at stuff for years, just messing around. But this is one of the few times I've hit something."

Chad is a broad-shouldered man, balding, quick to flash the people he knows a grin from under his worn, smudged, black cowboy hat. Along with a muscled chest and arms, he sports a slight paunch, both traits gleaned from long seasons spent cutting Douglas-fir in the Pryors, hauling it back to Red Lodge, and as often as not, selling it by parking the load in front of the Snow Creek Saloon and waiting at the bar for customers. Though born and raised in Montana, Chad can't really be described as a good old boy, at least not in the usual sense. Like a number of forty-something men in these mountains, he's at various times been a ski goon living for fresh snow, a carpenter, a cowboy, a devoted follower of that get-rich-quick pony ride that's forever booming and busting in the oil fields to the south. Up until now, if you'd have run into him some night in the Snow Creek or the Blue Ribbon, straight or twisted, as likely as not he might have struck you as a genial, even gentle sort. In the eight years I've lived here I've rarely heard anyone talk of Chad as being either overly sour or mean. His friends will tell you that the times he's bared his teeth and started barking all came after an accident years ago, when he was forced to dive out the door of a drilling truck with no brakes careening down a steep Colorado mountain road, smashing his head open against the pavement in the process, immediately after which the good doctor introduced him to a muley mix of pain-killers so full of kick he ended up popping them long after the pain had up and left. But on first meeting, or second or third or even fourth, a mean streak probably wouldn't be something you'd suspect.

In truth Chad shouldn't have even been in these sagebrush hills today. Wouldn't have been within five miles of wolf number Ten had he not been out yesterday looking for bear at the foot of the mountains and gotten his truck stuck in that grease that forms above Scotch Coulee every year about this time. After which he walked back down the road to the house of an old friend from high school, Dusty Steinmasel, made arrangements to shuttle another of his own trucks back this morning to pull out this one. It was shortly after pulling the truck free that the two men spotted Ten on the top of the hill, that Chad pulled out the rifle and looked through that scope, pulled the trigger, blew him away. While at his trial the prosecution will suggest that Chad did in fact know what he was shooting at, that's a question that'll never be fully answered. What's perhaps most outrageous is that after the two men walk up the hill and discover that yes, this really is a wolf, they drive over to Belfry for a twelve pack of beer and then, at Chad's insistence, come back and grab the wolf carcass, skin it out and take the head, carry the booty ten miles to Chad's house, drive back to Dusty's, all the while with the collar sitting in the back of the pickup still transmitting location signals. More evidence, many will claim, that Chad is a staunch member of the local screw-the-feds club. Then again, it could be just another example of the guy's almost child-like tendency to be forever in the moment, with no thought of what might wait around the corner—a little-boy trait that at its best makes Chad worry free, quick to forgive nearly any sin against him, and at its worst leaves him at the mercy of some dark and dangerous whims.

* * * * *

Wolf number Nine, mate to the animal that Chad McKittrick just shot, is waiting near an old fire trail some five hundred feet above the Rock Creek Valley, on the steep flank of Mount Maurice, amidst dark runs of spruce and Douglas-fir, aspen and lodgepole, and clumps of wild rose. There are wet places tossed across this side of the mountain, springs and seeps that give rise to rich runs of meadow grass and thickets of willow and alder—miniature versions of the kinds of discreet habitats wolves often use as rendezvous sites beginning in late June, when members of the pack come together to take turns feeding and caring for the pups. The deciduous trees are still weeks away from leafing, and in the right places Nine can look north through openings and see the town of Red Lodge nestled between two windswept benches, just over three miles away.

Of course we can't know what mood, what bent of feeling might be wrapped up in Nine's waiting. From a practical standpoint wolves

are adaptable creatures, quick to adopt a new game plan in the face
of changing conditions. But they're also among the most socially
attached of animals, bonded to one another in so many obvious
ways, quick to act for the benefit of another member of the pack.
Biologist Dave Mech has compared the relationship between the
wolves of a pack to that which exists between a dog and his master.
So strong, so overt is the society of wolves that some native cultures
claim to have patterned their own social structures after them: the
behavior of the alpha pair having launched the notion of shared
governance, where leaders strive to control while still leaving an array of decisions to others, the rooting of child care in the extended
family. At the cost of anthropomorphizing it's hard to imagine that,
at the very least, Ten's absence isn't causing Nine if not exactly worry,
then at least occasional pangs of unrest. Who knows? Maybe the
feeling is something akin to what Ten experienced standing on that
hillside in a snow storm above the Rose Creek pen, waiting for his
mate to walk out and join him in the wilds.

    Finally Nine can wait no longer. She makes her way downslope
from the fire trail across patches of foot-deep snow, slips under the
low-lying branches of an old spruce. She's been here before, in this
dark place, crouching on the east side of the tree trunk thoroughly
hidden from the world, digging with her front paws through the
thin layer of duff down through the cold black earth to the warmer,
more insulated layer of humus, creating a bowl-shaped depression
some three feet across and ten inches deep. A birthing bed. Several
weeks later, lying on my belly under these very same branches, the
first thing I notice is how the side of the tree next to that bed has
been worn smooth, the outer bark completely stripped from long
minutes spent rubbing against it with her back. Even more interesting is the fact that the ends of all the twigs within easy reach of the
bed have been thoroughly chewed off. Was it just to get them out of

her way? Or is this a wolf's version of biting bullets in the throes of labor?

36   Meanwhile, confusion is lying down like a spring fog across the recovery team. First Nine and Ten disappear from the northern reaches of Yellowstone. Then when the signal from Ten's radio collar is finally picked up during an overflight it appears to be coming first from inside the town of Red Lodge, then west and later east, all without there ever being the slightest hint of the wolf himself. During all this, Nine's signal indicates she's continuing to stay well to the south of Red Lodge, more or less in one place, suggesting she may be denning. And yet given the stresses of relocation, the thought of wolves having bred and now being ready to whelp is in itself just short of incredible. Shortly after Ten's collar starts giving off a mortality signal (the blip of the transmitter pulses faster if an animal becomes inactive for a prolonged period), Steve Fritts, Joe Fontaine, and Ed Bangs with U.S. Fish and Wildlife decide it's time to go looking for his mate. "If something happens to her," Joe Fontaine tells me, "we'll want to be able to go in fast and get those pups."

       This is a big deal. Very big. These are likely the first pups born in the Yellowstone ecosystem in some seventy years, and right now pressures from wolf opponents are threatening to scrap the entire rest of the reintroduction. Add to that the fact that whatever kind of help the wolf recovery team decides to offer Nine, it will be their first management action, and as such, heavily scrutinized. On April 27th Fontaine is out on foot in twelve inches of snow along that old fire road south of Red Lodge, radio receiver in hand, looking, listening. "I'm walking down the hill, trying to be real quiet, and all of a sudden I hear this little squeal. It's a weird sound—something more like a bird than a wolf. So I keep going. I get a little further down and I find a place where the female has bedded down on the snow. And that's when I hear the whimpering of the pups." Fontaine lifts up the spruce bough and sure enough, there they are, just a day or two old, eyes closed and huddled together in a tight ball. He does a quick count—it's hard to tell whether there're seven or eight—turns tail and gets out of there, not wanting to keep Nine away from her young any longer than necessary.

Shortly after this discovery, Fish and Wildlife launches a feeding effort, mostly haunches of deer carried in and left along the fire road, which gives Nine the option of either dragging the meat down to the den or gorging herself and then regurgitating it for the pups. The fact that this meat is road kill being taken from area highways is kept a secret. "There's always the chance," Fontaine explains later, "that someone will go out and drive the roads, lace all the carcasses they find with strychnine."

In the hours and days after finding these pups, confusion yields to high anxiety. Can Nine really raise this family all by herself in that location? Every time she leaves they'll be open to predation. Furthermore, the chance that another male might come along and adopt the pups—something wolves do quite willingly—are slim to none. Even so, while U.S. Fish and Wildlife sees the urgency of the situation, they also seem hesitant to intervene in what they feel should be a hands-off operation. Ed Bangs in particular is reluctant to micro-manage this project, and going in and trapping a female and her eight pups and transporting them back to the park can in one sense be looked at as just that.

Planted squarely on the other side of the teeter totter is Park Service project leader Mike Phillips, who seems about as willing to wait for something to happen to these animals as he is to start passing the hat to raise money for the newly established Chad McKittrick defense fund. With each passing day Phillips pushes harder to get mother and pups back. The feeling I get talking to Mike is that he's going to make this wolf thing work come hell or high water, just as he helped make it work with red wolves in North Carolina, and eight pups born to million-dollar adults the first season out of the gate is a big part of the recipe for success. If one of his wolves gets in trouble, or for that matter causes trouble, this is the guy who's going to want to catch it and bring it back, dotting every "i" and crossing every "t" along the way. Unlike Fish and Wildlife, Mike does see the value of micro-managing, at least to a point, especially in the early years of a project when he's trying to build a base of knowledge. Tweaking things when necessary, tuning this and that for the sake of learning what works and what doesn't. "Two hours in the office for every hour in the field," he likes to say, referring to what he sees as the critical job of documenting everything that could have the slightest relevance to this effort.

But beyond all that, sometimes I wonder whether the predicament of Nine and her pups reminds Phillips—as well as every other project staff member in the park—how they themselves sometimes feel venturing out for a burger or a beer in someplace like the Road Kill Cafe in McLeod, or any of a hundred other places around this ecosystem: like refugees in a war zone, stuck behind enemy lines. Plain and simple, the general feeling in the Park Service is that when Nine's pups start roaming they stand a very good chance of being killed, and not just by other wildlife. "Even that collar tossed in the ditch like that," Doug Smith says, talking about finding Ten's radio collar at the edge of a culvert, still intact. "I don't know. It seemed like a slap in the face. Kind of a 'Ha ha, I killed this wolf. What are you going to do about it?'" (During the trial Dusty Steinmasel will claim his tossing that collar in the ditch was actually a subtle way of helping the feds out, so bad was he feeling about what Chad had done. Personally, I find neither explanation likely, both requiring a measure of intent and forethought beyond what Dusty or Chad seem to have in their pockets on any given day.)

In truth there have been documented cases of female wolves successfully raising their young alone, especially in areas of abundant prey and relatively low populations of other wolves. Thirteen years ago a male alpha was shot north of Glacier National Park, leaving his partner to care for seven eight-week-old pups on her own, which she succeeded in doing. Likewise, in 1990 a male wolf in western Montana was able to rear a half-dozen month-old pups on his own after humans killed his mate. But those kinds of stories are likely the exception, probably best thought of as striking examples of how wonderfully adaptable wolves can be in the face of hard times. There's no getting around the fact that the increased danger of obtaining food as a lone animal, combined with having to at least on occasion leave pups completely unguarded, makes this a very risky business. More typical of the way things might go is the tale—related by wolf biologist Rolf Peterson—about a female wolf on Alaska's Kenai Peninsula trying to raise at least seven pups on her own, and all of them dying by autumn. During the last observation of those pups, sometime in late August, researchers found them to be only about half the size they should have been.

The end of the week comes and Fish and Wildlife is still brooding over the issue, and Phillips is ready to detonate. To him the hesitation seems less a matter of thoughtful pondering than simple lack of vision. Every day that passes is like hot peppers on heartburn, bringing all the things he detests: hesitation, indecision, lack of planning. In fact it drives him so nuts that he can't seem to keep from breaking that sacred rule of not lifeguarding at another agency's swimming pool.

At this point it's easy to imagine that Fish and Wildlife might be at least tempted to drag their feet over this issue simply because of what they see as Phillips' growing heavy-handedness. Maybe some of it has to do with the fact that Mike is the new kid on the block.

And in a field where the territory of biologists tends to be every bit as guarded as that of the wolves they study, there are times when nothing is less welcome than another charismatic alpha male. On the other hand, no matter what kind of territory a wolf biologist may have staked out, these days he's likely to be under constant attack from politicians and special interest groups—a fact that leads some to be either extremely cautious or protective about what they do.

Despite bad feelings the players in both agencies are well aware the clock is ticking, that the debate needs to be resolved because there's a fine line they'll soon cross when it'll be more and more difficult to round up pups. Young wolves get smart awfully fast. There's no getting around the fact that the bigger these pups get, the harder they'll be to catch.

For that small, loud group of locals who have been expecting the worst out of wolves, Nine setting up house in the area is the first piece of proof that the invasion is underway, that Carbon County is the chosen turf for marauding bands of cattle-killing, pet-eating, child-nabbing predators, the first county in Montana to be re-conquered by God's great mistake. A couple of those people I talk to, though, seem to be wrestling with a disturbing, even haunting question. Had Ten not been killed, would this pair have ended up back in Yellowstone and given birth there instead? Was Red Lodge just the end point of one of those rambling round-trips that are especially common around denning time, just like happened with the Crystal Bench wolves a few weeks earlier? Clearly there are those among the recovery team, including Mike Phillips, who think these two would have probably denned on Mount Maurice anyway, a notion based on the fact that signals from both wolves were heard there during earlier flyovers. Yet returning to Yellowstone, even very late in the game, wouldn't have been out of the question. There are records of female wolves taking off on jaunts of nearly thirty miles, only to crawl into the den the next morning and give birth to a full litter of pups.

Likely scenario or not, if you hate wolves it's a terrible "what if" to even think about. That instead of having nine of the things camped at the edge of cattle country—a mother and eight pups— had that shot not been fired there might not be any. Of course there are always other, more effortless ways of looking at it. Like the solution offered by two locals I sit next to on a cold afternoon at the Lost Village Bar in Roberts, who grumble their disappointment that old Chad didn't just keep on going, that he didn't find a way to kill them all.

* * * * *

The next time Joe Fontaine leaves meat for Nine and the pups he notices she's followed his earlier tracks back up the mountain from the den site for some thirty yards, sniffing them, investigating, assessing the danger they present. Unknown to anyone, though, what she concludes from this intrusion is that her makeshift den under the big spruce tree just isn't safe. Sometime after that first encounter, perhaps on a dark night covered in clouds, Nine grabs her pups and one by one carries them for roughly half a mile across a cold, spring-fed freshet, up a steep run of mountain bristling with dark groves of spruce and lodgepole, finally reaching a gnarly sprawl of boulders and lichen-covered talus. To and fro, twisting through the black timber eight times that night and back again, one pup at a time clutched firmly in her mouth, none of them ever making so much as a squeak or whimper. For safety she may avoid open areas, like that small stream corridor leading up toward the talus, favoring more cloaked routes through the trees.

Though there's almost certainly a strong sense of purpose to her movements, it's easy to imagine that all in all she's managing this task fairly calmly, weaving back and forth through the hushed forest, having figured out exactly what to do and now just doing it. Kind of a striking contrast to the recovery team, struggling to get a handle on all the possibilities, the risks and potential consequences of performing such a complicated rescue; trying to anticipate well ahead of time all the things that could go wrong.

At last the agencies forge a plan—in part, perhaps, thanks to a fragile peace engendered by the long-standing friendship between Wayne Brewster at Yellowstone, and Ed Bangs with Fish and Wildlife. Mother and pups will be captured and relocated back to the park, placed in the same pen at Rose Creek that Nine walked out of with her mate and yearling daughter just eight weeks before. The option of placing Nine back in the acclimation pen at Rose Creek, as opposed to simply letting her and her pups loose on their own, reflects not only biologists' preference to play father wolf and bring in food, but also the fact that there's no guarantee a female wolf under these kinds of stresses might not just lose it and walk off, abandoning her pups. Since the operation will take place outside the park, Joe Fontaine will be in charge. Some in the public at large are denouncing the action, claiming blatant over-tinkering by the feds. Curiously, they include a few of the same people who, when Nine and Ten were first discovered near Red Lodge, lambasted the feds for not doing a better job keeping the wolves in the park.

The plan is to capture Nine first, then with her safely kenneled go back in for the pups, and finally helicopter the whole family back to Yellowstone. Things get rolling on Monday, May 15th, and by Tuesday it's obvious that more meat is needed in order to be sure of luring Nine into one of five leghold traps being set near the old fire road, not far above the den site under the old spruce tree. Doug

Smith gets a phone call in Yellowstone, is asked to grab radio telemetry equipment and some carcasses from the park's walk-in freezer
full of road kills, then drives over the next day to join the effort.
Once the trap transmitters are in place signals are checked, both
from the Super 8 Motel at the south end of Red Lodge where the
crew is staying, as well as from an old dirt wagon road east of the
den site. The team also starts monitoring the comings and goings of
number Nine.

The capture will be done with leghold traps, modified so the
jaws close only tightly enough to hold Nine's foot in place until the
workers can reach her. In addition, each leg hold trap has a cord
running from it to a magnet taped against a radio transmitter sitting
in a tree; as long as that magnet is in place, no signals are emitted
from the transmitter. When an animal wanders into the trap (or a
deer or moose stumbles across the trip wire or the tape falls off in
cold weather), the magnet comes loose and the transmitter starts
giving off signals. The crew then hears the signal, jumps in the trucks,
heads up the mountain. That added bit of technology goes a long
way in improving the odds of success; without the quick response
time allowed by the transmitter there'd be a greater chance of Nine
escaping, or hurting herself fighting the trap, or even getting into
trouble with a bear or some other predator that happens by.

Joining in the operation almost by accident is the owner of the
Super 8 Motel, Gene, who I don't think could be more thrilled. He's
nearly giddy, like a kid who just woke up and glanced out his window to find Michael Jordon shooting baskets in his driveway. He
treats the biologists and veterinarian Mark Johnson like Nobel lau-
reates. Before Mark and Doug Smith arrive, Joe Fontaine takes Gene
up on an offer to have his night staff monitor the signal receiver;
understandably, the clerk isn't well versed in the art of signal monitoring, which is unfortunate, because one night the battery in the

receiver goes dead and no one picks up on it. Thankfully it's not a night when number Nine happens into one of the traps. When Smith and Johnson get to town, they begin monitoring the transmitters themselves every two hours, then trade off in the dark hours, Doug listening at midnight and Mark getting up at two and four o'clock in the morning. Finally, at 4:00 in the morning on May 18th, a half-asleep Mark Johnson hears the signal they've been waiting for. He wakes up Doug Smith who verifies it, and the two men rouse the others. Because the team doesn't want to drug or otherwise handle number Nine in the dark they shower, pour down some coffee, take a cold breakfast, finally arriving at the fire trail just after dawn. Mark spreads a ground cloth near the vehicle and lays out his equipment—stethoscope, thermometer, scale, blood tubes, needles, vaccines—while Joe and Doug and Carter Neimeyer walk the trap line to look for Nine.

As it turns out she's caught in a trap set by Carter Neimeyer, which contained as an attractant a scat from her mate, big number Ten, collected while the wolves were still in the pen. She's generally in good shape—85 pounds—and her mammaries are filled with milk. Her lower left canine tooth is broken, though, her upper left second incisor is gone, and some of her other teeth show considerable wear—all of which is likely due to relentless chewing on the chain link in those first weeks of captivity. Such tooth damage is actually present in a number of the Yellowstone wolves, and is probably the most lasting physical consequence of the entire reintroduction. (Remarkably, while still in Canada a group of researchers listed one kenneled wolf as a sub-adult, in part based on tooth wear, even though the day before other researchers recorded him as a pup. The short of the story is that it took just twenty-four hours of chewing on that steel to significantly wear the sharp edges of his teeth.)

Nine gets a new radio collar, has a blood sample taken, is vaccinated for common dog diseases such as parvovirus and canine distemper. Finally the team photographs Nine's teats in order to document their size during lactation. Such record-keeping is a good reminder of how much we've yet to learn about wolves; these photos may one day be a valuable reference for someone who catches a female wolf and needs to verify whether or not she's lactating. Once the processing is finished, veterinarian Mark Johnson decides against bringing her out of sedation. Instead she's placed inside a plastic kennel in a shaded van and allowed to sleep it off; her head comes up for the first time just as the helicopter touches down nearby. Now the only thing left to do is gather the pups, load them and mom aboard the helicopter, and head for Yellowstone. The den site is well off the fire road and wrapped in a ragged curtain of brush and timber, and proves more than a little difficult for Joe Fontaine to find again. He tramps back and forth through the woods for some twenty minutes, growing more and more agitated, cursing himself for not having marked it more clearly in his mind. Of course everything looks much different than when he last saw it, when these woods were wrapped in a foot of snow. Finally a lucky break hits, and Mark Johnson and Gene drop down at just the right spot, landing at the old spruce tree with a tremendous sigh of relief. They pull back the lower branches, stare into that dark furrow, look at each other in disbelief.

The pups are gone.

FOUR

Spring is also coming home to the Lamar. Warm breezes puff out of the west with all manner of good smells on their breath, herding great rings of cumulous clouds through a sky of forget-me-not blue, rippling through mats of Timothy in the lowlands, as lush as I've seen them in years. From a distance the valley bottom looks like a grand run of horse pasture on some vast, long-forgotten estate, the grounds being quietly claimed by sage. Over near the Specimen Ridge Trail a golden and two immature bald eagles gorge themselves on the fresh carcass of an elk. Milling about on the greens are herds of bison, their tired, ragged patches of wooly underfur yielding to smooth hair the color of cinnamon. Some of the bigger adults stand in the meadows and push at one another, neither animal moving much, looking like Sumo wrestlers angling for a take down. About a dozen baby bison are visible now, among the first of the season, running and bucking like rodeo stock, maybe not quite believing how much fun it is to have legs. A few days ago zero hour came for a pregnant female right as she was crossing the highway, so she simply laid junior down in the middle of the road.

With the Soda Butte group having set up house along the

Stillwater, as May unfurls it's the Crystal Bench animals that begin taking center stage for the wolf watchers of Yellowstone. Despite making a mad dash to Red Lodge, traveling some twenty-five or thirty miles a day over rugged, sky-scraping terrain and then apparently returning to the park by the same route, for the most part they seemed to have settled smack dab in the middle of that stretch of real estate researchers thought would be such a perfect home for wolves. The most shocking thing about it is how incredibly visible they are, spending much of their mornings and evenings just south of the Lamar River feeding, traveling, and sparring with everyone from grizzlies to bison, all within easy sight of the highway. In a bar in Gardiner a member of the wolf recovery team shakes his head, stunned that the Crystal wolves would be going about their business in such plain sight, even if there is a good-sized river between them and the growing number of watchers along the highway. It's the kind of surprise that can astound even rational-thinking scientists, make them start reaching into the shadows—at least in safe company and after a couple bottles of beer. "I don't know if it's just pure luck," he says. "Or maybe it's all those blessings from the Native Americans. But being able to see these wolves so often, that's a real gift. Something we should be especially grateful for." Indeed, as the weeks unfold, Joe and Jane Tourist from urban New Jersey will stand as good a chance of seeing the kinds of wolf-related events that biologists in places like northern Minnesota have invested years to witness.

The next night, on the way back from Cache Creek, the pack wanders into the backside of nearly a thousand elk. For almost three miles the sub-adult wolves test the herd with a spirited chase or two, like rebel cattle dogs making off with the master's livestock. On occasion the movements of the wolves cause the elk to split in great, flowing waves of hooves and sand-colored hides. "It looks like

Denali," Bob Landis says. "Here it's elk. There it's caribou." This kind of prodding of elk, bison, bear, or moose seems especially appropriate for young animals that will soon have to become masters at spotting vulnerability. Running the herds is what allows wolves to draw out the problems that exist in individual animals, to force even a slight lameness or other weakness to reveal itself through the stress of exertion. Wildlife veterinarian Mark Johnson recalls a mentor who once told him that one of the best ways to observe wildlife diseases in a herd is to pay special attention to the animals clustered at the rear; it's there, he explained, you'll find the one or two that may have a bit more trouble breathing because of an old pneumonia, or are slightly slower, perhaps due to a leg injury. It's not hard to imagine these wolves doing just that.

The return of wolves to greater Yellowstone is an event that will forever change—many would say restore—what modern science has come to accept as the normal dynamics of this ecosystem. These blustery initial encounters between wolves and other species are the first whispers of how elk, moose, and deer will react to wolves over the course of the coming years. On Isle Royale moose cows with young calves like to hang out in campgrounds, or in other places occupied by people—the last place you'd find any respectable wolf snooping around. Will the same be true in Yellowstone? Will early season campers at Pebble and Slough creeks wake up now and then to find moose staring in the windows of their pickup campers? In the mid-1980s wolves began recolonizing Canada's Banff National Park, some thirty years after they were extirpated as part of a rabies control program. The bighorn sheep there reacted to that return by once again hanging out near steep ledges and precipices—so-called "escape terrain"—whenever the wolves were near. Will those magnificent bighorn that tend to hang out on the north edge of the Lamar Valley near the Buffalo Ranch do the same?

50

And what about Yellowstone's elk? Some speculate that the herds may end up moving more, especially on early summer range, when calves are young; already this spring there are days when the Lamar Valley herds seem to be huddling in tighter clusters than in years past. Eventually, as wolves spread into other areas of the park, there may also be changes for elk wintering in geothermal areas. While the animals in large thermal basins could probably still outrun wolves, what will happen to those used to hanging out in the smaller thermal zones? Will wolves force them out into deep snow, where they can make relatively easy kills?

Of course it isn't as if Yellowstone's prey animals are starting from scratch. The bulk of responses to wolves by deer, elk, and moose will be second-nature—a matter of relying on the same anti-predator instincts they used for centuries to keep from ending up as lunch not just for wolves, but grizzlies, mountain lions, and coyotes. Deer fawns and elk calves will continue to be closeted away in thick blankets of vegetation, protecting them when they're most vulnerable simply by hiding them from view. Some elk will continue to show a strong preference for avoiding brushy areas and willow thickets, unwilling to chance a surprise attack.

An equally fascinating part of the wildlife puzzle is trying to figure out who will benefit from the presence of wolves. Bears, of course, are only too happy to come across wolf kills. The carcasses wolves leave behind are likely to become a significant new source of food, especially in springs that follow light winters, when oftentimes there isn't much laying around for bears. Even now, following a relatively late winter that left a decent number of carcasses, grizzlies have already been seen feeding on three of the sixteen wolf kills marked so far. Also add to the list of beneficiaries bald and golden eagles, ravens, magpies, foxes, and wolverines, to name just a few. These days even chickadees can be seen feeding on the fat of wolf kills, treating such carrion like so many hide-covered suet feeders.

Coyotes too, of course, are showing a great penchant for grabbing dinner at the nearest wolf kill. At most of the Crystal pack kill sites, for example, somewhere off in the distance you'll nearly always see coyotes, sitting and watching, waiting until the wolves have had their fill and wandered off so they can trot over and help themselves. And yet this is dangerous business. In the months to come researcher Bob Crabtree and his assistants will document a number of coyotes being chased and even killed by wolves, some ending up suffering a rather gruesome death stretched between two wolves in a deadly tug-of-war. As for encounters between wolves and coyotes unrelated to disputes over carcasses, right now those consist mostly of yearling wolves giving short chase, occasionally followed by at least one bold coyote chasing right back. In time the wolves seem to tire of such games, and simply lope off to some new adventure elsewhere. Back in April I remember feeling kind of sorry for a group of coyotes when the Soda Butte pack turned tail after a brief game of tag. Just up and left the playing field. The coyotes sat down on their haunches, looked after them, barked and yelped and yowled. Then again some might say that was a victory of sorts, that those howls were the last word from the winners; the coyotes, after all, had held their ground.

If coyote numbers go down as a result of fights with wolves, as some biologists are predicting, other parts of the ecosystem will feel the effects. Pronghorn would almost certainly benefit from such declines, since right now they lose extraordinarily high numbers of fawns to coyote predation every year. Drops in coyote numbers may also end up having effects on small mammals; populations of red foxes, for example, may increase significantly.

* * * * *

The wolf watchers are holding their breaths, some so buzzed with excitement I half-expect them to wet their pants. At a cluster of old dens along the south side of the Lamar River, burrows that have been used by local coyote packs for years, Crystal's alpha pair is digging, as if the time was coming for this female too, number Five, to bring new pups to Yellowstone. Even well before these excavations, when the wolves were still in the pen, researchers noted that Five had blood on her vulva, a sign of proestrus. Some of the security rangers guarding the pen even saw her exhibiting classic breeding behavior: averting her tail in front of her partner, even being mounted by him for a few seconds, though she was never seen engaged in the ten-to-thirty minute copulation tie normal to breeding.

"I would have thought the coyotes would be standing around trying to bark them off," says Bob Landis, who has spent uncounted hours over the past ten years getting to know the song dogs (coyotes) who dug those den sites. "But there's no sign of them anywhere. I don't know, maybe just having a pen full of wolves nearby for nine weeks was enough to send them packing." It's true that many of Lamar's coyotes showed no end of concern through the early winter months when the wolves were penned here. At the time, Bob Crabtree found that coyotes living in areas immediately adjacent to those acclimation pens vocalized far more often than did coyotes elsewhere; in fact, rarely would a single hour pass without them letting loose a rousing chorus.

In all, the Crystal wolves have been seen excavating in five separate places spread out across the old stomping grounds of three different coyote packs; several are near the Crystal Bench acclimation pen, and two others are further east, past the mouth of the Lamar River canyon. On June 3rd, at the home den of the Norris Peak coyote pack, five Crystal wolves will get into a fifteen-minute tussle with four coyotes; eventually the coyotes will give up the den, losing a pup in the process, and all five wolves will take turns excavating the site. All of which continues to make the watchers think Crystal's alpha female is about to whelp; the constant pawing of dirt, the way she crouches in the openings, a Goldilocks trying to find just the right birthing bed. At one site Five spends just under an hour working and fussing, actually disappearing into the hole and backing out again. Later the four subordinate animals in Crystal go off on their own, as if heading out to hunt, leaving the alpha pair at the entrance to the potential den site, the female digging and the male lying close beside her. Spectators stand poised along the highway, talking in whispers, the cameras rolling and clicking. Much to their disappointment, after a time the alpha male, number Four, leaves the site and heads up the valley. Ten minutes later the alpha female follows.

On leaving that site the pair wanders near an elk herd that's been in the area for the past two days; soon they begin moving toward a certain cow, taking on that careful stalking position that precedes a kill. Why they end up choosing this particular animal is hard to say. Maybe it's just not stepping as lively as the other elk. Or there might be an unnatural hesitation in the animal, spawned by the fact that it hurts to run. The wolves may even pick up on subtle, abnormal positions of the animal's ears, which might suggest it's focusing on some pain it has in its belly or hind legs. One of the effects of wolves having been gone from the ecosystem for more than sixty years is that a higher percentage of debilitated animals, perhaps just like this one, have been able to survive when they otherwise would not.

When it comes to making kills, wolves actually strike out far more than they succeed. For one thing, most of the time healthy large animals that stand their ground will avoid being attacked.

Furthermore, if the threat is real and flight seems to be the best response, healthy adults of most prey species can—except in deep snow— outrun a pack of wolves. And yet even in those times when running turns out to be the right thing to do, it's common for elk or deer first to merely watch, studying the wolves, holding back until it's obvious they're under attack. Unlike humans, who tend to re-main in full panic as long as the perceived threat is still in sight, elk are likely well aware of the rules of the game. Which is why you often see them grazing in the same pasture where wolves are feeding on one of their herd mates. While that may seem strange, when you think about it this is a terrific piece of survival strategy, allowing them to save energy for the short, considerable burst of speed they'll need to get away when there really is a reason to run. (Also, unlike a deer in the forest, an elk living in the open, sprawling lands of Yellowstone would never be able to stay out of sight of predators anyway.) Likewise, as soon as wolves stop chasing, the prey usually stops running, a habit that allows them to recover faster, lest there be another encounter later on. As far as that goes, wolves aren't much into wasting effort either. Once the chase begins, unless there's clear evidence they're actually gaining on a prey animal, they're quick to give it up.

This time the kill is simple, fast. The Crystal alpha pair walks up together toward the elk, and as they close in, the female, number Five, rounds the back side. In one rather seamless, orchestrated move she locks her jaws onto the hindquarter of the animal well ahead of the rear leg, while her mate takes hold of the throat; a burst of wres-tling and in less than ten seconds the elk is on the ground, dead a few seconds after that. It's rarely so easy. Some kills require an extraordinary amount of energy, running at full speed for several minutes and covering a mile or two of uneven terrain, and then even more intense effort to actually make the kill. After feeding, the alpha pair heads off into the timber to lie down for a while, replaying that age-old pattern in wolves of gorging and then resting. The next day they're back, feeding again. Later a wandering grizzly picks up the scent, decides to head over for a few bites of his own, ambles away.

55

Though on occasion the Crystal Bench pack was seen taking a bite or two from winter-killed animals they happen to find poking out of the snow, on the whole they've shown a strong preference for meat on the hoof. "That's interesting to me," says project biologist Doug Smith, who has a long history of working with wolves in northern Michigan and Minnesota. "In other places I've been, any meat seems like good meat to wolves." Maybe they're celebrating the sudden, sheer abundance of fresh meat in this park, especially after nine weeks in the pens where there was nothing but convenience food in the form of partially frozen road kills. (Well, there *was* that suicidal fox that Mike Phillips thinks may have climbed up and over ten feet of chain link on the Soda Butte pen and dropped in among the pack. Not much meat on that guy, though the wolves definitely got every morsel they could. To this day Park Service photographer Jim Peaco likes to think of that fox hanging nervously off the top ridge of a pen panel, the wolves waiting down below with their paws out, calling up to him: "Come on, buddy, we got ya.")

When the wolves were in the pens, researchers added to the amount of food they'd normally get in the wild, increasing it from the roughly ten pounds per animal per day that wolves in good circumstances average on their own, to fifteen. This had to do with the fact that animals in the wild eat and then walk off and rest for long periods, often fifteen to twenty hours, just as the Crystal alpha pair is doing now; in the pen, though, these same animals tended to follow up dinner with long bouts of restless pacing along the chain link, actually using more calories than they would if they were out on their own.

At this point biologists have documented fifteen elk, one moose, and one mountain goat killed by Yellowstone wolves, all of them either calves or older animals in advanced stages of malnourishment. "They're not random killers," Doug Smith reminds a gathering of people at the annual meeting of the Greater Yellowstone Coalition. "They're selective killers. They're just doing what wolves do." In fact it only makes sense to kill weaker, more vulnerable animals whenever possible, given that an adult wolf can be quickly maimed or killed by the slash of hooves from a healthy elk. In truth there's really only one predator that shows a preference for taking the strongest animals, the prime breeding stock. And he's got a gun.

* * * * *

It's hard to watch the comings and goings of the Crystal pack without being impressed by the individual animals, especially the alpha pair. Number Four, the male, while a good ten to twenty pounds lighter than his two fellow alphas in the other groups, sports a wonderful, rich charcoal coat with a singular patch of gray splashed across his chest, the color of aspen smoke, and a grayed muzzle. Though an older wolf, there are yet days when he struts around as if his main job in life is to be thoroughly full of himself, which in a way it is. His tail is held high. It flows, like some kind of royal banner blowing in a fair-weather breeze. Contrast that to the sub-adults who carry their tails much more carefully, controlling them lest they hold them as high as number Four and end up being put in their place. The female, on the other hand, number Five, sports a striking blend of blonde and gray fur. Like her mate she too carries herself freely, and yet she seems less overt about it, less commandeering. Of all the wolves now running in the park it's this alpha female that has the most striking presence, the clearest lead over her group. Even in the pen she was the first to feed after workers dropped off food, often hours sooner than the rest of Yellowstone's wolves. Likewise, when the recovery team would leave after feedings, some of the security rangers noticed her breaking away from the rest of her group, who were all busy pacing in the comfort zone, and heading over to within five or ten yards of that gate, pausing, looking at it. When the pen gate was finally opened on release day, a remote video camera showed her to be the first one bold enough to come close to that opening, doing so some six times in twenty minutes, staring out through the hole, as if she was the one charged with the job of trying to figure out what it all meant.

Since release Five's been the one in command, deciding the when and where of the pack's movements. Sometimes she runs lead as the pack makes its way up or down the Lamar, while her mate keeps an eye on things from the rear. But even when she's not in the lead, she's still leading. As wolves often do, this pack tends to travel in scattered clusters. Though another animal may actually be in front at any given time, when they reach some unseen fork in the road it will be Five or sometimes her mate that moves off in a new direction, leaving the others to pick up the change, which they do almost immediately. Rolf Peterson tells of watching a pack of wolves from the air on Isle Royale. Traveling in a straight, fairly tight line, suddenly the lead wolf stopped and looked back, at which point the alpha female stepped out of the line and set a new course of travel. No matter how scattered the rest of the group gets, more often than not Five is able to rally them quickly, even from the outside edge of spotting-scope distance, where you see her head go up and only a few seconds later do you actually hear the bay of her howl.

So far the offspring of this pair consists of the four male subadults running with them today—one gray colored much like a coyote, and three blacks, their dark coats making them wonderfully easy to spot as they lope across the distant benches of the valley, or better yet, while playing with one another on the lingering patches of snow—something they do a lot of these days, often stopping every few hundred yards for a good game of wrestling or tug-of-war with an old bison bone. One of these black yearlings, number Two, holds the record for the amount of time needed to give up the acclimation pen; while it took some ten days for his pack mates to leave the pen for good, it took him eleven. Once out and away, he spent almost the entire month of April off by himself, then hooked up with his pack again in early May, joining them on regular east-west runs along the open swales of the Lamar, back and forth to Cache Creek. Since that time Two, while still part of the pack, has often headed off for brief periods to do his own thing, returning to the group at his pleasure.

While none of the wolves have yet preyed on bison, the Crystal pack yearlings have a remarkable fondness for sparring with them. On May 11th the four yearlings are lagging well behind their parents, moving more reluctantly than usual—even though mom and dad are calling them in—and end up stopping to push around a small herd of about ten bison. Though the bison have their tails up, all in all these big ungulates seem downright casual about the wolves, as though they wouldn't be going anywhere if they hadn't felt like running anyway. Some suggest that such sparring by wolves is really an indication of their desire to hunt; that over time such casual, almost play-like engagement with potential prey animals adds momentum to that urge, like athletes psyching up before a big event. Maybe so. Fifteen minutes after the bison bout comes to a close, the four yearlings take a cow elk. On one occasion four bison bulls seem to have had just about enough of this whole wolf thing, and suddenly run over as a group to stand on the mound where Five has been digging out her fifth hole, looking like trained bouncers at the first whisper of a bar fight, sending Five scurrying off across the meadow. The bison cow and calves nearby seem to take this as a sign that troubles may be escalating, and they too trot off into the hills without looking back.

59

Beyond the antics of the yearlings, as a rule the Crystal pack simply drifts past clusters of bison without giving them a second look. Sometimes the wolves probably just aren't in the mood. Then again this lack of engagement may also have to do with the fact that adult bison are such formidable opponents; there are a number of researchers who report watching a lone bull bison making an aggressive move toward a full pack of nosy wolves and sending the whole bunch scattering. Even here in Yellowstone it's not unusual to see bison clustering around their young at the approach of wolves, forming a mean, snorting wall of muscle that no critter playing with a full deck would try to break through. One of the few places where wolves dine regularly on bison is in Wood Buffalo National Park, in northern Alberta, and nearly every animal taken there is either a calf or an older, weaker adult. It's probably safe to say that from the time a bison reaches maturity to the beginning of physical decline, she's very close to being invulnerable.

Brawn and muscle aside, there's an interesting question about whether or not Yellowstone's wolves even recognize bison as a potential food source. One of the reasons biologists selected these wolves from around Hinton, Alberta, was because they were used to preying on elk, which is also the principal prey base here in Yellowstone. Some thought that this would be an influencing factor on day one of the release—that by giving wolves quick, easy access to familiar prey right out of the pen might just encourage them to stay put. Wolves seem to learn what's worth eating and what isn't through a system biologist Steve Fritts has called prey imaging.

Basically this means that wolves select what prey to pursue and kill by watching what their parents and other pack members kill. Through this process wolves may well form what Fritts calls a "search image" for that prey species; animals that don't fit the search image, then, are pretty much ignored. This may be part of why in Minnesota, western Montana, and across much of Canada packs of wolves are continually strolling right past herds of cattle without giving them a second look. It isn't that cattle couldn't serve as prey—clearly, there are some wolves who do break the search image and end up lunching on livestock. But the vast majority simply don't seem to recognize cows as a source of food.

When you think about it, such a strategy makes a lot of sense. Being a predator, after all, is a deadly occupation; as a wolf it's clearly to your advantage to stick with those animals you know, with what's familiar. Wolves that have preyed on elk for generations understand how they will react. They know how elk move when the pack enters their flight zone: the speed, the reflexes, the specific dangers of slashing hooves. They know how the animals can be killed—where bites are best placed to bring them down. To our way of thinking, it would seem easier for wolves to take slower, less agile animals, like cattle. But they don't know cattle. And on the whole, it's wolves reluctant to go after species they don't recognize that survive best. (That said, it's not a bad idea to have at least a few experimenters in the ranks, since there's always the chance of something wiping out the normal prey base.)

As the days wear on, it becomes clear that while Crystal has in many respects turned into the perfect wolf pack, one thing they will not do this year is give birth to pups. Maybe, as scientists suggested all along, the stresses of being penned for those nine weeks kept the pair from breeding. As for number Five's restless ways, her pawing at so many likely den sites, that may be related to a not-altogether-uncommon phenomenon biologists refer to as pseudopregnancy. Evidence so far suggests that pseudopregnancy is the result of elevated levels of prolactin, a hormone present in a variety of species, including alpha male and female wolves. (That alpha status may be an important distinction. For example, the cycles of certain hormones having to do with reproduction can be suppressed in subordinate females; remove the alpha female from the picture, though, and that cycling resumes.) Prolactin, which tends to rise naturally in the spring around the time of whelping, is thought to initiate maternal and paternal behavior in alpha wolves—causing them to do things like dig dens, and to show fidelity to a specific birthing site.

In the weeks to come, still another theory will be tossed out to explain the lack of successful breeding by the Crystal alpha pair. It has to do with the idea that Four and Five may be father and daughter. Dave Mech's DNA studies on some two dozen breeding wolf packs in Minnesota find that, when given a choice, alphas just don't breed with animals that are closely related to them. In closed systems like Isle Royale, of course, where there's been a total lack of immigration by new animals for decades, there's no choice. Which may be why, according to researcher Rolf Peterson, you see some alpha pairs there go years without any breeding activity at all. "I think all those wolves on Isle Royale would love you if you dropped in a few new animals," jokes Doug Smith. And yet the four yearlings running around in the Crystal pack today are supposed to be the offspring of Four and Five. If those two are in fact father and daughter, they must have either been placed in a position that encouraged them to breed last year despite a natural reluctance to do so, or else—and this seems unlikely—the biologists didn't really capture the alpha pair.

All in all it's another mystery that may never be solved. "It seems there was an era in wolf research when a lot of pigeonholing was going on," says U.S. Fish and Wildlife biologist Steve Fritts, "when we were making a lot of blanket assumptions based on the behavior we observed. The last ten years has been about whittling away at those generalities, about finding exceptions to the rules. And when it comes to wolves, there are a lot of exceptions."

FIVE

It's hard to imagine a more terrible moment. Wolf number Nine secured in the kennel box, coming out of sedation, the pups out there somewhere in this thick, steep tangle of timber and brush, the clock ticking. If the pups can't be found, Nine will have to be set free and the entire process started again. And of course the next time she'll be trap-wise, so much so she may be impossible to catch at all. Doug Smith pulls from his pocket a group of aerial photos taken from earlier tracking flights with Mike Phillips, during which Nine was located hanging out not below the fire road but well above it, close to a small, secluded drainage capped with a jumble of talus. Dick Martin has been called in with his tracking dogs, and is on the way. In the meantime Mark Johnson, federal tracker Carter Neimeyer, Doug Smith, and pilot Rick Sandford head back to the road. Time to regroup. Take a breath. Get heads screwed back on straight. Stay off the mountain so as to not contaminate the site, possibly ruin it for the tracking dogs.

Joe Fontaine and Gene, meanwhile, are above the old den site, fidgeting. When the waiting becomes too much, they decide to walk west to a small creek that drops down the mountain in a series of pools, head upslope from there, try to find the area identified in the aerial photos. The two men continue climbing the steep flank, eyes glued to the ground, patient and frantic at the same time, Joe making soft, breathy grunting sounds over and over again, mimicking the call female wolves often issue to their pups on returning to the den. In one spot well above the fire road Joe finds wolf scat—comforting, in a way, and yet all but worthless. Some two hundred yards above the fire road they finally land at a steep jumble of talus, and there the search continues among basketball- to wheelbarrow-sized rocks, into and out of crevices packed with gravel and ice, past boulders with eight-foot-high faces of smooth granite. At one point Fontaine offers one of his wolfy grunts, and this time there comes back a muffled noise—something that sounds a lot like the whimpering of pups. The men approach, trying to move quietly, to be as nonthreatening as possible, but the little ones suddenly jolt with fear—astonished, perhaps, that those grunts not only didn't belong to mom, but didn't belong to anything that looks, sounds, or smells like a wolf at all. The pups grow quiet. All but one, that is—an alpha in the making, Joe calls him—a little muchacho brave enough to toss off a round or two of some rather terse chatter before clamming up like his brothers and sisters. "And then there's just no noise from them at all," Gene says. "Just cowering. And these eyes—the bluest eyes you've ever seen—looking right up into our faces."

As wolf homes go, this second den site isn't exactly typical in that there's no hole for Nine to actually crawl into. Still, it's an awfully good spot. There's a long, flat patch of earth hidden from the downslope view by an enormous boulder where Nine can lie and nurse her pups, while on the other side, to the east, is a sheer, overhanging wall of gray granite, offering good protection from sleet and snow. Immediately adjacent to this is a tumble of rocks and boulders with all sorts of holes and crevices—perfect for times like this, when something strange and scary comes along, when what a kid needs even more than mom is a darn good place to hide. At Joe's approach the pups squirrel themselves into these pockets, some of which are capped by enormous slabs of granite; when the rest of the crew arrives on the scene a lot of effort is spent dismantling this rock puzzle in order to reach the hiding places. With a little patience and a lot of long arm, one by one six black pups and one gray are gently lifted out—cowering, confused, probably wishing hard for mom.

While at this point you can cut the relief with a knife, there's still something troubling the capture team: Did Joe Fontaine see seven pups on that first hurried visit to the spruce tree den three weeks ago, or were there eight? Anxious to make sure they're not leaving anyone behind, several of the men take turns lying down in front of one of the dark crevices where several of the pups had been hiding, pushing in their arms, fingers extended, feeling around for the slightest touch of fur. The problem is that no one can quite manage to reach all the way to the rear of the burrow. Grabbing hold of a blunt stick, extending the reach a little more, they do end up making contact with something soft tucked into a crevice at the extreme rear of the cavity. But is it a wolf, or just dirt or leaves? Growing anxious the men grab hold of lanky, six-foot-two-inch, one-hundred-eighty-pound Doug Smith like a battering ram and literally wedge him into the opening up to his neck. Straining for every inch of reach he can muster, Doug's fingers finally touch what is most certainly fur. No doubt about it, there's another pup inside. The problem is that, while Smith can touch the animal on the forehead, he can't even begin to grab hold of the little guy and pull him out. Scratching his head to come up with something to extend Doug's reach, Rick Sandford reaches in his pocket and brings out a leatherman's tool—a compact, knife-sized device that includes among its parts a pair of needle-nosed pliers. Crude as it may be, the tool

66

provides the extra four inches of reach Smith needs. And out comes number eight. All in all, he seems only slightly worse for the wear—just two small breaks of the skin on his forehead above the right eye, each about an eighth of an inch long, which veterinarian Mark Johnson treats with antibiotic salve. Remarkably, through this whole terrifying assault, the poking and pinching and manhandling, the little pup hasn't made a sound.

This is the moment, then, that will long be remembered. Right here in front of this stony jumble on the steep shoulder of Mount Maurice, six grown men jumping up and down, grinning, slapping one another on the back, pushing huge sighs of relief through their lips and down the mountain through the spruce and lodgepole, toward the budding cottonwood leaves that line the icy waters of Rock Creek.

To get the pups back down to the fire road Gene takes off his coveralls, ties knots at the bottom of the legs, zips the zipper, and presto, the perfect wolf pup bag. Once down to the road, the animals are then transferred to two Tupperware-style plastic containers, four to a box, and carried out to the truck. They too are processed by Mark Johnson: weighed, vaccinated, and given a physical exam, a small amount of blood taken for genetic marking, then all placed carefully into a plastic kennel. Johnson has already visited the helicopter to get a sense for what kind of seating arrangements might work best. In the end the team decides to remove the back seat of the aircraft and slide mom's Vari-kennel box crossways into the rear of the helicopter. This leaves a long, narrow tunnel between the forward panel of the kennel box and the vertical wall behind the pilot and navigator seats. This gets lined with a sleeping bag, and then Johnson simply lays the pups one at a time at the mouth of the tunnel, allowing each one to scurry inside. "It was like putting them at the mouth of a den," he says. "They all ran to the back, huddled together in a ball, and didn't move."

And with that Johnson is off to Livingston, hoping to finally care for an abscessed tooth that's swelled the entire side of his face for two days straight. Gene is back to caring for tourists at the Super 8. And Doug Smith is off with mom and pups in a whirl of rotor blades, bound for Yellowstone. The ordeal at Red Lodge is finally over.

67

In the weeks to come there'll be a lot of confabs about how best to handle these nine wolves—in particular, how long to keep them penned. How long before pups can hold their own against coyotes and other predators? Having no real territory of their own, what's going to happen the day this group comes face to face with wolves from another pack? Amazingly, a day or two after their return, number Seven, Nine's yearling daughter from Canada, travels all the way from the northwest corner of the park to within a half-mile of the Rose Creek pen. Once the workers stop shaking their heads in disbelief, they start crossing their fingers that she'll stay. Because no matter what happens from here, this is one single mother who could use some help.

* * * * *

The next time I see Chad McKittrick is on May 20th, three weeks after the shooting, at a ranch near Willow Creek. The bluegrass and wheatgrass are coming back with bells on, stretching for the spring sun, painting these heavy, treeless hills in the colors of carrot tops, like Irish moors. Three horses led by a free-thinking Arabian have broken loose from their home pasture and have taken to the crest of a long swell east of the ranch house, running up there in twisted lines backlit by the rising sun, flouncing like conquistadors. The owner of the ranch has called Chad for help. "When it

68

comes to calming nervous horses," he tells me, "there's not many people better than old Chad." Before the roundup the three of us sit for a time at the kitchen table, Chad pulling on his third or fourth bottle of Zima, Verlynn and I breaking out an early bottle of Budweiser, talking about the shooting of number Ten.

There's something different about Chad this morning. Regret and anger and bravado are wrestling one another in a crowded room; that, and knots of fear, pulled tight as a new fence. One minute he's praising the feds for how well they treated him, railing against them the next, saying how they've tapped his phones and are following him everywhere he goes, how they'd better watch out because all he has to do is give the word and his brother will cause them big trouble. He assures me that nothing will come of the shooting, that he'll be let off, but those claims are always followed by flashes of panic, re-kindled whenever he thinks about doing time. At one point he stands up, leans on the table, looks me straight in the eye. "It was an acci-dent, man" he says. "I didn't know it was a wolf. Dusty can say otherwise but he's a liar. And liars end up in hell." Whether or not that question is ever resolved, it's worth noting that there was a time not long ago when I heard Chad talking in favor of wolves coming back, if not exactly to Red Lodge, then at least to Yellowstone. The fact is wolves fit nicely into fancies about living life elbow to elbow with a wild, uncivilized place. Like grizzlies, cuss them as some people may, wolves can be a touchstone that allows people like Chad to stay connected to a fermented old love for a West that still turns on dark woods, bad weather, and long, gun-toting trips through the backcountry on ornery horses. In that sense he's not much different from the trappers and woodsmen I've run across in Canada and Minnesota; even those who don't like wolves would rather live in country with wolves in it.

Around noon we head outside to deal with Verlynn's runaways.

"You know," Chad tells me as we make for the barn, "I heard they sedated those wolves in the pens. That's the only reason they weren't violent in the park." He says it in a tone of voice that suggests he doesn't really believe it, but that he sure would like to. I tell him I know the veterinarian who's been in charge of the animals, assure him that there was never any such drugging, but he ignores it. No doubt someone did tell Chad such a thing. Actually it fits perfectly with the other fantasies of the day—most of which aren't Chad's just yet, but soon will be. Like the one where Canada refused to give us any wolves except those that were proven stock killers, and our government went ahead and took them anyway. That's my favorite. It points to the real core issue about this reintroduction—the fact that much of the rage running across these hills isn't about ranchers perceiving wolves as a threat to cattle and sheep. While livestock may be the kindling, the real fuel for the burn is that the federal government is behind the project. In a wolf-related story in my local paper, the ranch wife of a county commissioner tells how her husband used to say he was proud to live in America. "But now the government tells you what you can do and not do. It's not America anymore." Wolves. In truth Westerners couldn't buy a more perfect evil if they rode straight to hell with a saddlebag full of cash.

The horses are still on the hill well east of the house, scattering then rushing back together again, like water parting around some invisible island; the Arabian looks down at us looking up, tosses his head, stomps one of his front feet. Chad studies him for a while, not saying anything, then assigns Verlynn and me standing positions along the entrance road from which, when the time comes, we can hoot and holler encouragement for the renegades to do the right thing and run back to the barn. Chad takes off his shirt, hitches his jeans, grabs his bottle of Zima, and begins a slow walk up the hill. He talks to the horses long before he gets there, and while I can't hear what he's saying, after a couple of snorts and back steps the Arabian visibly relaxes, saunters over to him, lets Chad rub his neck and whisper some sweet nothing in his ear. A minute or two of this and Chad gives an easy heave onto the horse's bare back, and just like that he's riding him back to his regular stomping grounds. The other horses simply follow along, like Chad was some kind of equestrian pied piper; I stand in my appointed position, watching him ride by, feeling altogether unnecessary.

Despite Verlynn's thanks and offers of "well done," Chad hardly seems pleased. On dismounting he mutters a cryptic "shit," puts on his best "that figures" scowl, lets loose a barrage of tired-sounding sighs. Verlynn's six-year-old son Cheyenne is with us, and several times Chad kneels down and talks with him up close, eye to eye, asking about school and how his horse and dog and cat are doing. Cheyenne, normally bright and gregarious, has known Chad as long as he's known anyone. But today he responds quietly, tenuously; sometimes I catch him looking at Chad out of the corner of his eye, as if something has changed but he doesn't know what. Maybe it's the intensity with which Chad is asking his questions, probing, urging responses, desperate to go hook, line, and sinker into this kid's world—a place that seems more sane, more light-hearted than the one now gathering around him.

When I leave in mid afternoon he's got nothing to say and I wonder if he's pissed at me for dredging up the whole damn sordid event on a day when all he was trying to do is forget. But there will be no forgetting, not for a long time to come. When the feds came to Chad's house and served him with a search warrant, he was cordial, sometimes joking with them, at one point even stepping outside with special agent Tim Eiker to hit golf balls off the side yard while the other agents went off and rounded up the wolf hide from the upstairs of his unfinished house, right where Chad told them it would

be. "Maybe this'll end up as one of those made-for-television mov-
ies," Chad suggested to Eiker. "Maybe I'll be famous." And he will
be, in a strange, sordid way. But on a local level his fame will be
forged less from the act itself than from the way he's beginning to
stumble, fast and often, a man caught in the glass like a deer in
headlights, uncertain which way to jump, finally choosing to leap
toward the very thing that's about to run him down.

SIX

The Suburbans and Winnebagos, the Jeeps and the Fords and the Subarus crawl along the Lamar Valley in the dull light of dawn, finally pulling off the side of the road west of the old Buffalo Ranch, so named for having once been used as headquarters to cowboy a dwindling bison population back into healthy herds. Where a month ago a fresh layer of grass grew, now in June tires and feet have worn away the vegetation and packed the ground into hard-pan. Those who have been here before, the veterans, pull in close beside the car next to them, knowing that in another thirty minutes the place will be packed with some forty or more vehicles. Lights are doused and doors creak open and owners stumble into the chilly air clutching tripods and spotting scopes and thermoses of coffee, smiling, offering quiet but excited greetings to those they recognize from having been here yesterday, and the day before, and the day before that. A few of the newcomers look apprehensive. They hold their arms across their chests and hunker against the thirty-degree temperatures, staring at the smears of snow still lingering in the high pockets under Specimen Ridge, maybe trying to figure out how freezing their butts off in the middle of nowhere before the sun is even up could possibly qualify as a vacation. The regulars, on the other hand—those for whom this has become something of a ritual— well, they look to be at the top of their game.

74

"Looks like clear sailing," Ed from Sacramento calls out in his loudest whisper. As usual he's armed with an enormous, two-thousand-dollar star scope which he'll use to scan the hillsides, finding all manner of grizzly and elk—and yes, on most days wolves—only to yield it to a waiting line of excited neighbors, some who have spotting scopes of their own but absolutely none who has one quite like his. You can tell Ed is awfully pleased about his role, more than happy to help, perhaps thrilled that this is one of those very few toys middle-aged men like himself buy that actually turns out to be worthwhile. He says in truth he brought the thing all the way from Sacramento to Yellowstone to watch the stars. No light pollution here, he explains. But as late night temperatures dropped into the twenty-something range his wife and friends bailed on him, leaving him to shiver out under the firmament all by his lonesome. Then with the wolves being so visible, well, it couldn't have worked out any better if he'd planned it. "At first we were just coming for a week," he tells me after spotting the day's first pair of grizzlies. "We've got a family cabin up in Silver Gate. But we talked it over and decided we're going to stay most of the summer. I mean what could be better than this?"

Club Wolf is in bloom. As it has been every day for the past several weeks, two hours or so at dawn, two at dusk, rain or shine, blue sky or fog. And while some of those living in the park regret the loss of peace and quiet in the Lamar Valley, it would be hard to fathom a more perfect setup for visitors. Unfold the camp chair or lean against the warm hood of your car, grab the spotting scopes and binoculars, and settle in for one of the greatest shows in the temperate world. Not only regular, almost daily sightings of wolves, but bison and elk and antelope beyond the counting, as well as frequent views of both black and grizzly bears with spring cubs. For some of these visitors, this experience has been nothing short of an epiphany about how to vacation in a national park. Before wolf watching, their routine was the same as it is for thousands of others: stop in at the visitor center and pick the brain of a naturalist to find out how to see Yellowstone in three or four hours—an approach that doesn't exactly lend itself to savoring the ecosystem. But hidden in this slow, simple waiting for wolves has been the chance to witness the gentle ebb and flow of wildlife, to hear the bright dawn swell of bird song, to revel in the way first light pours into the wrinkles of the land.

A yearling grizzly is offering up fine entertainment this morning, engaging in a loping, hopscotch chase after a sandhill crane, the bird rising and settling back down again just in front of the bear several times over hundreds of yards, the bear finally stopping and looking around, bewildered, as if wondering how in the world he ended up there. Framing the stage on either end of the valley are isolated patches of fog, drifting slightly, swallowing up whole herds of bison and then releasing them, like a sigh.

Several of the wolf watchers are still talking about the special treat they had last night, something not seen before. One of the black yearlings from the Crystal wolf pack was wandering around not far from a pair of grazing pronghorn and, not being too familiar with such a creature, somehow got it into his head to try to catch one. With an explosive kick of his hind legs, he broke into one of those fast, ears-back-in-the-breeze runs. Impressive, really. One of the pronghorns lifted his head casually, watched the yearling's approach, and when the wolf was about forty feet away the two of them simply looked at one another, then fired off like bottle rockets across the meadows and over the distant ridge south of the river, leaving wolf panting in the grass.

No wonder these people are thrilled. Mary Anne Bellingham from Billings—M. A., as she likes to be called—has been here with her ten-year-old daughter, Brynn, nearly every day for a month now, for the most part living and camping out of their Suburban. Up every morning at 5:30 to watch for wolves, then out hiking and geyser watching, then back in late evening for still more wolves. Most days Brynn is still very much asleep when the Suburban starts rolling down the Lamar Valley, though she has an uncanny ability to wake bolt upright at the sound of her mother's voice calling out animals: "Coyote ahead. Moose in the meadow on the right. Bison on the road." And of course the comment that gets the quickest rise: "Wolves are out." M. A. is the one Club Wolf member who always keeps the tripod under her spotting scope set at kid level, not just for Brynn, but for any other little person who happens to be around. "The adults get so carried away when they see a wolf," she explains. "Sometimes they forget all about giving their kids or even their spouse a look." M. A. came to Yellowstone a couple times when she was a kid living in Missoula. Years later she met the man who would be-come her husband here (up Cache Creek, a favorite haunt of the Crystal wolf pack), got married at Old Faithful on a winter day at forty below, and still she can't seem to get enough. It isn't that these wolves are magic to her—some kind of spirit guide, as they seem to be for some—but more that this is the first summer of their return, which makes it a rather incredible historical event. And M. A., whose 1907 Victorian home is filled with virtually every book on Yellowstone ever written, is a remarkable fan of history.

On the day the Crystal wolves walked out of the pen M. A. celebrated by buying a tape of wolf howls and sitting up in her kitchen listening to it, over and over. In a sense you might say she tends toward making memories with her ears. "One thing I'll always love about this summer are the sounds of this valley. From now on, every time I hear a sandhill crane, or that low grunt the bison make, or meadowlarks singing, I'll think of the wolves coming back to Yellowstone." Those same sounds are floating across the valley even as we speak, backed up by the yips of a half-dozen anxious coyotes, a wildlife chorus, warmed up and letting loose, singing the sun up over Amethyst Mountain.

A few minutes later I overhear M. A. telling stories to a young couple from Utah—their first day at Club Wolf. "A month ago we saw them take an elk calf," she's saying, talking fast, nervous with excitement. "You could see the alpha female stand on the carcass, urinate on it. Then later the younger ones got in there and fed, were like playing tug-of-war with one of the bones. When the wolves left one of the yearlings had the bone in his mouth. Just took it with him." The Utah couple acts as if she must be the luckiest wildlife watcher on the face of Yellowstone. They nudge closer. Maybe they're thinking that wolf watching is something like fishing, where you try to hang close to somebody who has just the right ju-ju to render fish helpless to resist whatever they throw off the side of the boat. "No, no," she reassures them when they tell her they haven't had much luck watching things in the past. "You wait and see. Keep watching and you'll see them. We've watched them, what, about thirteen out of fifteen days now."

Still, the couple seems unsure, like it's going to take an act of God to shake them out of their curse of showing up the day after the best of everything. I'm almost glad M. A. doesn't tell them about last week, the time when three of the Crystal yearlings exploded out of the aspen trees, the black one in the lead carrying a half-eaten elk calf carcass in its teeth, only—a few seconds later—to have an incensed two-year-old grizzly run out of the woods after them. About how the yearling carried his stolen prize into a patch of conifers while one of his brothers, the gray, turned on the bruin and went nearly snout to snout with him, just a few feet separating the two animals—the wolf, satisfied he'd made his point, finally walking off into the woods to get his share of the goodies. And then how bear approached those same woods and yet another yearling wolf rushed out to engage him, this one trying to distract him, to lead him away. But bear kept his eyes on the prize, headed into that forest to get his breakfast, walked out ten minutes later empty handed.

All this with sixty or so people gathered at the overlook, swelling fast to nearly a hundred, until there was an honest-to-goodness wolf jam the likes of which this park has never seen. Meanwhile Park Service interpreter Rick McIntyre and his assistant, a sixth-grade teacher from California named David Gray, were sweeping their spotting scopes along with the action, calling out the play by plays like sportscasters in overtime, trying to cycle through the dozens of frenzied bystanders who didn't have equipment for a fast fifteen- or twenty-second look. And the bystanders themselves—people of all ages, from Florida and Michigan and Japan and Holland—looking at one another with open mouths and wide eyes, laughing and grabbing arms and slapping the backs of strangers standing next to them, some clearly feeling chosen, others not believing their eyes. After watching the bear encounter, one guy in his twenties from New Jersey just shakes his head, apparently wondering if he'd been had by some Disney-style trick of the Park Service. "Animals don't do that," he says. "Do they?"

By and large these gatherings have a taste of the international to them. Like the three twenty-something couples from Germany in that rented motorhome over there, the group with the men who during the past week have become such dependable spotters. Each day the guys stand out in the chill of morning and scope the valley to locate the wolves, and when they've found them they run back to the motorhome to alert their wives, who are sitting inside with the babies. But there's also a surprising number of people like M. A., locals, some who haven't been to Yellowstone in thirty or forty years. People from Livingston and Dubois and Pocatello and Big Timber, many getting up at two or three in the morning so they can arrive at these overlooks by dawn. And while some have actively been pushing for wolf reintroduction for years, a lot more simply read about it in the paper and decided to come. "I've always wanted to see a wolf," one man in his seventies from Livingston says. "Grew up on a ranch up along the Shields, and they were gone from that country in pretty short order. When my dad was young he even did some bounty hunting up around Grass Range. Just doing what needed to be done. But he was a little sad about it, too. Didn't know he was helping to wipe 'em out."

To be able to sit beside a paved road in a plastic web lawn chair and watch some of the first wildlife encounters with wolves is without question among the more remarkable gifts to humans in this thoroughly enchanted year. More than any other events—more than the occasional soulful howl loosed in the dark of night, more than yearlings wrestling one another and playing king of the mountain on remnant patches of snow—these first encounters between wolves, their prey, and other predators are what burns into my memory. They're the sights that steal breath, that make the sun stop in the sky. On one level it's the first spin of a fresh, fascinating wheel of animal behavior; on the other it has the spark of something ancient, of relationships thousands of years old, fanned back to flame before our eyes.

The undisputed leader of Club Wolf is Park Service Interpreter Rick McIntyre, a serious, forty-something man with a sense of humor dry as the high desert. Rick has seventeen years of wolf-watching experience under his belt, having made some five hundred sightings in Alaska's Denali National Park, and another fifty or so in Glacier, in northwest Montana. So driven was he to interpret these Yellowstone wolves for the public that in an unheard-of move he actually went out and raised the funding for his own position from private donations. "This is an incredible time for Yellowstone and for wolves," he says. "I really wanted to be here." McIntyre admits that before coming to the park he would've counted himself lucky to see one wolf in the wild all summer long. But of course things worked out a little better than that. "Here it is not even July, and I've already had 119 sightings. And all of those were right from the park road."

When asked about his favorite sighting experiences, Rick offers pretty much the same answer as a lot of other Club Wolf members, not to mention filmmakers and scientists. "The play," he says. "Those Crystal yearlings have spent so much time at it. Playing tag, ambushing one another, that kind of thing. One of the yearlings has this wonderful habit—when he's feeding, just for the fun of it he'll rip off a piece of the carcass and toss it in the air, wait a second, and then leap completely off the ground and catch it. It's just like a dog leaping up to catch a Frisbee.

"And then the visitors," McIntyre continues, suddenly flashing an uncomfortable, embarrassed look. "Most of these people are seeing a wild wolf for the first time in their lives. And when that happens, well, some of them seem to feel the need to hug the nearest government official, which happens to be me. I mean let's face it, in today's climate there aren't too many times where government workers get hugs from citizens." Indeed, in the coming week a couple in their sixties from the Midwest will be struggling for five days straight to catch sight of a wolf, without any success. In fact they'll keep canceling their departure, adding one day to their vacation and then squeezing out yet another, until they just can't stay any longer. When, in the last light of their final night in Yellowstone Rick spots a yearling wolf and points it out to them, the woman will break down in tears, go up and give Rick the kind of kiss usually reserved for returning war heroes or firemen who pull little kids out of wells.

"There are times," Rick confesses, "when it feels like it's the early Sixties and I'm press secretary to the Beatles. Everything is just so overwhelmingly positive. Come to think of it," he adds, deadpan, "maybe we should release a CD of their howls from the Lamar Valley." In truth, sometimes all this enthusiasm for wolves can be a little much. By the middle of June it seems every wolf watcher in Yellowstone knows McIntyre's mini-van from a mile away. Many are the times he pulls off the road to take a leak—and remember, the poor guy's been drinking coffee since 4:30 in the morning— only to have six or seven cars full of excited people pull in right beside him, certain he must have spotted another wolf.

Like so many others, McIntyre considers this reintroduction an incredible success story, occurring at exactly the time the Endangered Species Act needed a big success. "It's amazing to see the joy, the incredible enthusiasm this reintroduction is bringing to thousands of people from all over the world. You wouldn't believe how many families have told me that when they heard the wolves were in the area they canceled all the rest of their vacation plans and decided to stay here instead." Of course that means money in the pockets of local merchants. The hotels and restaurants in Cooke City and Silver Gate are overflowing, and right now you could probably sell tourists rusted tin cans if they had a picture of a wolf scratched on them. Sales at the gift shop at Roosevelt Lodge are on their way to a whopping forty-four percent increase over last year, and the manager attributes the bulk of that to wolf watchers. Estimations based on work by University of Montana economist John Duffield

82

suggested this wolf reintroduction would bring some twenty-three million dollars' worth of extra business annually to the regional economy; if this summer is any indication, he may be right.

Back at Club Wolf again two days later, and still more grins and wows as one of the Crystal Bench teenagers, a curious eighty pounder, decides to engage a 2,000-pound bull bison. Spotting the bison lying in the grass up ahead chewing his cud, the wolf gets into crouch position and starts sneaking up from behind. From a distance he seems awfully good at this creep game, stalking with enormous care, getting closer and closer—first within long leap range, then down to a single three-foot pounce, the bison never showing any sign of being aware of his presence. Then at the last minute the bison calmly turns his head, flicks his tail, and suddenly wolf is bolting like he's been buck shot, fleeing full speed across the meadows south of the river.

One morning back in May a busload of fourth-graders on a field trip from Greybull, Wyoming, drives by, clueless about why such an enormous crowd of people would be standing around out here in the middle of nowhere. At the mention of wolves from someone in the crowd, the chaperone bristles; from the look on his face they may as well have said they were watching Satan. His bristle goes to full-blown blanch when Rick McIntyre invites them over to look through his spotting scope, and the whole class runs over screaming with excitement. M. A. is there to help out, resetting the tripod as one excited kid after another runs up to it, looks through the scope and spots the wolves, then accidentally kicks it as he dashes off to give someone else a turn. Incredibly, the kids even see the wolves feeding on an elk calf taken earlier that same morning. Later they write fan mail to "Ranger Rick" and sign the cover sheet "your enchanted friends."

"I want wolves in Yellowstone," Sarah writes. Though Sarah

and some of her friends had to work through some sadness about the taking of that elk calf, in the end she concluded that wolves need to eat, too. "After seeing them I decided it was a good idea," she continues. "I'm glad you reintroduced them."

83

Grant goes farther still: "I loved seeing wolves in Yellowstone. Wolves are my favorite animals. When I saw a wolf it was unspeakable. I will not write much in this letter cause I can not describe what I felt."

Toby's appreciation, on the other hand, tends toward the pragmatic: "I think the wolves in the park is a good idea because more people might come to the park and then you could make more money."

The fourth graders write their letters on paper with an ink drawing of a wolf face in the upper left hand corner. Shelbee draws a series of open circles leading from the wolf's forehead to a text balloon, like cartoonists use to show what a character is thinking. "I like it here very much," it says.

During the same week a teacher with a group of fifth and sixth graders from St. Louis visiting the park for an environmental education program happens to spot a letter to the editor in the *Billings Gazette* by Leon Carpenter from Lewistown, Montana. Besides predicting the end of the ungulate population, Carpenter chides the Fish and Wildlife Service for claiming that tourist revenues will go up because of wolves. "My experience," he says, "indicates that very few tourists, if any, will ever see a wolf." In fact, the day after Carpenter's letter appears, the teacher and his students get a rather different view of reality; back in St. Louis again, they decide to write a response. "Together with about 40 people we observed 5 different wolves feeding on an elk carcass for several hours. Nearby were other bison, pronghorn, ravens and a bald eagle. Later, with the wolves still in the area, 3 grizzly bears fed on the same carcass. We have been truly privileged to see something this special. For us, this experience represents hope for a return to harmony and tolerance with nature. Mr. Carpenter, we wish you could have been there with us."

While opinion in the northern Rockies for and against wolves seems somewhat tilted in favor of wolves, in a lot of places around this ecosystem it's easy to find yourself wondering if these animals have any fans at all. But that notion melts like June snow after an hour or two at Club Wolf, or on one of Rick's twice-weekly wolf walks, where a phenomenal 100 to 165 people are showing up every morning. As another part of his regular duties Rick drives to places like Tower Falls, takes a wolf pelt given to the Park Service by the Canadian Government out of his vehicle, drapes it over his arms, then starts casually walking through the parking lot, talking with visitors. I've never seen anything like it. It's as if there's some kind of mass consciousness going on; he literally can't get more than fifteen steps from his car before a crowd has pushed in around him like neighborhood kids running to an ice cream truck. Not just Americans, but Germans and Pakistanis and Japanese, French and Brazilians and English. Incredibly, in less than a month of such roving interpretation McIntyre has spoken to about 6,000 people, which will eventually grow to 22,000; by the time summer winds down, the attendance for all Rick's activities will be nearly 40,000. Out of all those people, fewer than ten will express opposition to the wolf program. Indeed, some visitors seem downright perplexed by the controversy. "Our refrigerator went out at the cabin last week," Ed from Sacramento says. "The repair man was this fellow from Billings, and out of nowhere he starts going on about the wolves. How they're the wrong animals, the wrong species, how it's all a big waste of money. We couldn't believe it. What could make a person think like that?"

If there's anyone at these gatherings who musters a measure of sympathy for those fighting against wolves, it's probably Rick McIntyre. "It's hard for environmentalists to understand what a rancher would have to complain about, why they'd have trouble taking money from a compensation fund set up by Defenders of Wildlife. But it's not so simple. Let's say you're a vegetarian. You spend all summer long tending and nurturing your vegetable garden, and right about harvest time someone's pet goat comes along and destroys it. You're not going to feel satisfied if the goat's owner says 'You lost ten heads of lettuce—at seventy cents a head that seven dollars; and those carrots, those would go for about fifty cents a dozen. Here's three dollars.' There's more to it than that. There's an emotional connection between a gardener and his crops, just as there is between a rancher and his livestock—an emotional connection that goes way beyond the market value of produce or stock."

Yet even compassion has its limits. When it comes to Chad McKittrick, neither Rick nor any of his faithful followers are willing to show a lick of sympathy. During his various walks and talks, people are continually coming up to Rick and asking what's being done about "the guy who shot the wolf." On strolls with the wolf pelt over his arm, some run to his side with worried, even angry looks on their faces, asking if this is the hide from the wolf that McKittrick killed. "You'd maybe expect that kind of thing from the people out in the Lamar," Rick says. "It only makes sense that those who take the trouble to find out where to go watch wolves might know about the shooting. But at places like Tower there's just a general cross-section of the visiting public. Even so, a lot of them know all about it."

*　　*　　*　　*　　*

The second week of July, and summer is wading in like a debutante through the knee-high Timothy grass, swishing up the

Lamar in a bright skirt of flowers, careless of the fact that snow continues to hang on in the north-facing pockets below Specimen Ridge. Rufous hummingbirds are arriving, hovering before orange-red sweeps of paintbrush, pausing there, as if not knowing where to start. Elk are leaving the valley, some going north, others climbing two thousand feet over the Mirror Plateau to greener, cooler pastures well to the south, near the Pelican Valley. Making this seasonal trek for the first time are dozens and dozens of calves, some old enough that at the first hint of danger they flee with the adults, while others, younger and more inexperienced, still rely on the strategy of the newly born, falling into a crouch position and holding their heads extended on the ground, perfectly still.

Elk seem to find great comfort in following familiar routes, and their travel this spring is along lines stretching back hundreds, if not thousands of years. As usual, several of the adults heading south are moving at a feverish pace, leaving the Lamar with what can only be described as a sense of urgency, perhaps pulled by memories of some other summer spent wading in those succulent pastures along the Pelican, feeding and growing fat in the grassy meadows of the high country. Indeed, the route to Pelican is itself a virtual smorgasbord of good eating. Mats of wheatgrass and fescue and tender bites of bluegrass; mountain dandelion, elk thistle, balsamroot, and on the cool, sweet banks of the freshets and in the aspen crannies, smatterings of columbine. Bistort and bluebell, hawkweed and monkeyflower.

The lives of the Yellowstone wolves will always echo the habits of elk, their primary prey base. And yet when it comes to following elk at this time of year, to an extent that proves to be a game primarily for packs like Crystal, which are free of pups. With Rose Creek back in the acclimation pen, the only free-ranging wolves with young in the Yellowstone ecosystem are the Soda Butte group. Research in other places has shown that once wolves with pups leave the den site in mid- to late June, they tend to move to a resting place—a so-called rendezvous site—where the adults can trade off care of the young. These tend to be safe, very protected sites, so much so that on occasion the rest of the pack may leave the pups altogether for brief periods in order to go out hunting in the surrounding terrain. At the first rendezvous site of the summer, the group can stay several weeks, after which they'll pack it up and move to a new location two or three miles away. As the season wears on, the stays at any given rendezvous site grow steadily shorter, while the distance between the sites grows slightly longer; by late summer the animals may stay a week or less in any given location. In later weeks the adults seem more prone to establishing sites near a recent kill. This way, instead of the adults having to carry food to the pups and then regurgitate it, the youngsters can simply feed off the carcass.

The late spring and summer movements of the Soda Butte group seem to match this more measured style of movement. In the early weeks of the season they trend southward from the den site at Flood Creek up the Stillwater, later moving slowly but surely west, toward Slough and Buffalo and Hellroaring creeks.

With no young to tend, the Crystal wolves have nothing to keep them from ranging at the slightest whim, and as a result are keeping in close and regular touch with the elk that left the Lamar and headed south, toward the Pelican Valley. And that means for the most part this group's almost daily performances south of the highway are over until November, after the flush and frenzy of the rut, when the ice and snows of autumn again press them back down to winter range. As for the human camp followers of the Crystal pack—the faithful members of Club Wolf—they keep at it awhile longer, dawn and again at dusk, then for the most part stop coming, departing the Lamar for more common attractions like Old Faithful or Lake or the riot of wildflower blooms building in the valleys of the Beartooths and the Madison Range. Finally making their way out of the area altogether, back to the lives they left behind in Los Angeles and Chicago and North Dakota; Europe, Germany, and Japan.

Thanks to generous rains early in the season, the Mirror Plateau is drenched in wildflowers. Yawning, grassy palettes splashed with the pinks of geraniums and the ragged scarlet of paintbrush. Exploring this high route to the Pelican I find myself rekindling an old habit of clocking the passing of summer by the opening of blooms and the setting of seeds—flax and camas for starters, on to columbine and fireweed, then goldeneye and coneflower and gumweed. Especially abundant this year are the lupine, blue as a twilight sky. Such a bumper crop seems appropriate, given that this flower takes its name from the Latin word for wolf and, in a few places, is to this day still known as wolfbean. More than likely the name comes from the fact that as the seeds start to ripen in late summer they produce poisonous alkaloids that can be dangerous to cattle; this danger passes, though, and by the time seeds are fully formed livestock can eat them without effect.

The departure of elk marks an important new time of the year for ungulates—a "safe zone" of sorts, when young are fully up and about, stronger, able to move freely with their parents. While that's awfully good news if you happen to be a young elk, deer, or moose, for Yellowstone's predators—lion to coyote, grizzly to wolf—it marks the start of greater challenges. Without the option of taking calves and fawns, every wolf pack, not to mention loners like that "dandy little wolf" number Seven, will be getting fewer easy meals, will be forced to work harder for dinners on the hoof. Now is when those wolf games, the pushing and poking at herds, looking for injured or arthritic animals, will really begin to pay off.

SEVEN

For all the weight of that dark moment when Chad McKittrick lined up wolf Ten in the scope of that 9mm rifle and pulled the trigger, as summer wears on he drifts farther and farther from regret. There are two strong camps of opinion gelling, turning fast to stone. One sees Chad as nothing but a wolf hater, someone who—as one woman, an old acquaintance of his put it—"should cut out the macho bullshit and start chewing for a while on how he'd feel being hunted down in the woods with a gun like a predator." People from outside the area, including almost everyone I meet in Yellowstone, are even less kind. Though none actually knows him they mince no words telling me how this guy is completely worthless, unfit, a redneck member of the Shoot, Shovel, and Shut-Up Club that wouldn't know the value a of wild thing if it bit him in the butt, at least beyond how its head or hide might look hanging on his cabin wall. For some of the locals, though, the sour feelings are more specific, centered on this thing they dislike in teenage boys and absolutely hate in the men who never outgrow it, this tendency to shoot at anything that moves—not because it might be a threat to livestock but because it's some kind of cheap proof that you haven't lost your aim. "I've yet to see a prairie dog or ground squirrel take a cow," one woman tells me. "But you sure as hell see a lot of them dead from target practice."

The other, more vocal camp is made up of those who, far from wanting to see Chad punished, would just as soon he be made citizen of the year. Some days it seems these guys are everywhere. Sitting next to me over breakfast at the Log Cabin, eating chicken in the Red Lodge Cafe, sipping coffee at the Ranch House. On Friday afternoons you can find them taking up at least a couple stools at the Lost Village Bar in Roberts, or huddled with bottles of Bud in the ever-present glow of Christmas lights at the El Rancho. Some, I get the sense, truly believe what they say. Others, including more than a few small businessmen dependent on agriculture, just plain like how it feels to be part of the club. But it's clearly those with the biggest ax to grind against the feds that are most determined to turn Chad into a poster boy for the anti-wolf movement, president of a club that six months earlier he would have just as soon spit on as look at. All across Carbon County they're slapping him on the back and buying him drinks at every opportunity, and in truth it probably feels like an easy way out, a welcome chance to bury the part inside that regrets the whole thing. "Shit," he tells me over the phone one afternoon. "All the drinks they're buying me, a guy could become an alcoholic in no time." Like many, I find what Chad did infuriating. Sometimes I stand in my back yard, look south toward Mount Maurice where those pups were born, feel cheated that I'll never have the chance to hear that family howl on winter nights, that I'll never know the thrill of crossing their tracks on my ski trips up the canyon. And yet, even with all that, it's still painful to see Chad being puppeted by this gaggle of dolts, to walk into a Red Lodge bar and watch him making deals with the devil in order to forget.

By mid summer he's all but unraveled. Unglued. And those who keep touting what he did as the act of a hero could care less. A wolf is dead. And that means we party. First he gets asked for a couple of autographs, then starts going out of his way to offer them to anyone and everyone in whatever bar he happens to be in. And these days he's in plenty. From then on there's no turning back. When we talk it isn't as if he figures he's going to fry anyway, and this is just a great way to live it up with what time he has left. Nothing like that. It's more like he's high on this roller coaster ride of a starring role, one that when tuned with the right mix of drugs can feel every bit as fantastic as that made-for-tv movie he dreamed about with agent Tim Eiker on the day he was busted. Day by day he's getting larger than life, right before his eyes. Before long he's donned pistols and a huge knife and is waltzing into saloons with t-shirts to sell: "Wolf Reduction Team," the shirts say, with silkscreened images of long bullets and a bloody wolf head. One night he struts into the Miner Saloon in Cooke City bedecked just that way; when the bartender jumps on him about the guns, tells him he can't walk around like that, Chad tosses back a disbelieving stare. "Don't you know who I am?" he asks. "I'm Chad McKittrick. The guy who shot that wolf." On the way home he wrecks his truck on the Beartooth Highway. "He was scary," said one of the guys called to the scene of the accident. "We honestly didn't know what he was going to do. He was belligerent, up and then down. Was he going to shoot at us, or what?"

And still more craziness. Surreal. A kind of Alice does Wonderland on cheap tequila and weed. A busy weekend at the Snow Creek Saloon in Red Lodge and Chad decides to ride his horse through the front door and into the crowded bar, pistol and knife strapped to his side like Pancho Villa without a cause, wrapped in one of those infamous t-shirts. The horse is nervous, of course—

snorting, halting. At one point his hooves slip out from under him and splay sidewise across the linoleum floor; were it not for the bar being on one side and a riser on the other the animal may well have gone down—maybe on top of Chad, maybe on those freaked-out college women from Minnesota, maybe on the owner of the bar, who by this time has smoke coming out of his ears. Finally led out the back, he circles around and tries again. This time they're waiting for him at the front door.

"It hurts," one of Chad's closest friends says to me. "I mean I supported him when all this first happened. Stood up for him. Now he just makes me look like a fool." The friend says he still cares, though. Still worries where all this is going to end up.

In mid-August Chad will be stopped on a dirt road outside Red Lodge and charged with DUI, possession of dangerous drugs, reckless driving, and resisting arrest, an event that sends most of his fair-weather bar friends scattering like rats off a sinking ship. As if that isn't enough, around that same time he goes a little nuts out at the old home place, driving around in a car, bare-chested in a black cowboy hat with a gun strapped on, setting up road blocks and harassing everyone from his neighbors to the Federal Express driver, berating them for speeding, telling them how they'd better watch out because he's the law now. (The Fed-Ex driver couldn't be coaxed back down that road for weeks afterward; neighbors with incoming packages had to drive in and pick them up at a clothing store in Red Lodge.) Finally he's rushed off to Billings for a psychiatric evaluation, loses his car, loses his guns. One of the final images I have of this strange, sad summer is of a bare-chested, dejected-looking Chad in chaps and a cowboy hat with bowie knife strapped on, riding his horse four miles from his house into Red Lodge, tying off to a neighborhood street sign, shuffling into the IGA with empty saddle panniers to fill them with groceries.

*   *   *   *   *

While Chad is waltzing himself toward destruction I decide to
head for Yellowstone, sign on to help build acclimation pens
for the next round of wolves coming in from Canada in January. A
year ago, when money was apparently easier to come by, the job of
building wolf acclimation pens went to the maintenance division of
Yellowstone Park, which completed the job of building three pens
in a little under four weeks, at a cost to the wolf program of some
thirty thousand dollars. Evidently this year those who hold the purse
strings aren't feeling very flush. When construction of two new pens
gets underway in early September the base crew consists of a handful of volunteers, and biologist Doug Smith—all of us eager to lend
a hand but none of us with a lick of experience. Fortunately we're
blessed with a fearless leader, Al Brower, the maintenance man with
a plan. Al is a Montana native, forty-something, a former railroad
worker from Livingston with a sly, arresting smile and more patience than Job. He's one of those quintessential Park Service
maintenance employees worth three times what he gets paid, a problem solver for even the most outrageous problems. After a few days
working with Al, I find myself wishing that those who so love to
hate all government workers, casting them as a bunch of slackers,
would put on a tool belt and try to go a few rounds with this guy.

Al shakes his head on hearing the plan to use volunteers for
building these two wolf pens, one on the Blacktail Plateau and one
up Nez Perce Creek. It isn't so much the lack of knowledge you get
with that kind of help, he says, but more that they tend to come and
go like loose change. He spends half a day teaching somebody how
to do something, only to see the guy bail out two days later when his
wife's aunt's sister falls off a ladder and kills the family dog, though
in truth it might have something more to do with the fact that

ten-hour days standing out in the heat pounding posts and twisting wrenches doesn't seem quite as glamorous as the notion of being a volunteer for the wolf program might have first appeared.

And then that little surprise on the first morning of work. Unbeknownst to either Al or Doug Smith, one of the Park Service interpreters has put out a major call for volunteers, going so far as to hand out flyers at campfire programs, soliciting in a manner more appropriate to massing a militia than for a modest construction project. On the first morning the parking lot at the Children's Fire Trail looks like Saturday at the flea market; more than forty people flock in, good folks all of them, from young, cool city kids shambling around in untied Nikes, to a seventy-something guy from Salt Lake City who tells me he'll need to take it a little easy because of that darned heart condition. For a second I think Doug Smith is going to fall to his knees and weep. But no. Rising to the occasion with a splendid show of generalship, Smith steps up and divides the ranks, assigns the bulk of the forces to about three hours' worth of trail clearing—basically removing debris along the route the mule-drawn sled will take next winter to carry in carcasses to the pen site—shoulders a roll of wire and a five-pound sledge, rounds up his pen builders, and tramps up the hill like Iron John to get down to work.

Within a couple days the group settles to a half-dozen regulars, and we fall together on that hilly knoll on the Blacktail Plateau like neighbors at a barn raising, hoisting 160-pound steel panels out of the morning frost, standing them up end to end and joining them with butterfly and muffler clamps, later securing the enclosure by standing on a ladder and driving steel posts around the perimeter, which is no easy feat in this rocky soil. Some sixty-five panels in all, including enough for a roomy isolation area attached to the main enclosure. This separate pen is to allow treating injured wolves without having to completely separate them from their pack, as well as for isolating any animal that might be getting beat up on by a dominant wolf who freaks in the stress of confinement and becomes overly aggressive. A curious feature of the main pen area is that it contains no square corners. For one thing, at captive centers wolves have been known to run up square corners like Marines assaulting a climbing wall. Also, these animals tend to pace the fence non-stop every time humans come around to feed, all the while half looking over their shoulders to keep an eye on the two-leggeds; corners, says pen designer Mark Johnson, would be just something else to worry about them running into and possibly injuring themselves. And finally, a lack of corners is another concession to the fact that, under the stress of being penned, dominant animals could become overly aggressive; a rounded pen means subordinate wolves cannot be cornered, and possibly harmed.

Once the vertical panels are up, a four-foot-wide apron of steel link is rolled out along the ground around the inside perimeter of the pen, then tightly laced to the bottom bar of the panels with steel cable that seems strong enough to hang a bridge from, and finally, snugged to the ground at its free edge by pounding in U-shaped pieces of iron reinforcement bar through the links. Wolves can dig like little backhoes if they think freedom waits at the end of the effort; without that curtain they might well end up tunneling themselves out long before the official release date. All in all these enclosures seem nothing less than fortresses, security compounds of the most maximum kind, a sobering reminder that certain things wild, including wolves, are made captives only with the most extraordinary effort. The theory that keeping wild wolves penned would help attenuate the homing response (that, along with choosing family groups in the first place) now seems almost irrefutable. Indeed, proving that theory this past spring with the original fourteen wolves has been one of the more striking accomplishments of this project. Still, the first couple weeks in these pens for creatures who run like the rest of us breathe, well, it must be hard. A bout of cold turkey the likes of which the rest of us can't begin to imagine. Even though veterinarian Mark Johnson designed these pens, though he fully understands and supports the need for this style of release, on some days they seem to leave him washed in sadness. Clearly such an arrangement is at odds with his philosophy as a wildlife veterinarian to minimize handling of any wild animal. "The ideal," I've heard him say many times, "would be to not handle wild animals at all."

At lunch, relieved to be on break after a morning of wrestling panels, we huddle from the heat in the shade of massive Douglas-fir trees, look out to the north and east across a sprawling thatchwork of nut-colored Timothy and huddles of aspen hung with gold, shimmering against the dark green of the spruce and Douglas-fir. This is classic nip and tuck country, a topography with the lilt and roll of heavy seas, the main memory bead on the rosary I use to invoke the magic of Yellowstone whenever I'm long away. As a wolf stuck in this pen, would staring out at that sprawling run of wild country soothe you, or just make you more eager to chew your way out and give it a go?

I'm sitting next to Al, and at one point ask him whether he gets grief from the guys he works with about helping out with the wolf project. "Oh, they can dish it out all right," he finally says. "So do a lot of my neighbors." The reason I bring it up is because of a story somebody told me a couple weeks ago, about going in to the maintenance shop to ask how long it would be before a certain job for the wolf project was finished. "I'll do it right now, for free," the guy answered. "If you'll just give me one shot."

To put wolves in these pens, of course, means having to feed them. Fifteen pounds of meat, per animal, per day. One thousand, four hundred and seventy pounds per week for the original fourteen Yellowstone wolves; about fourteen thousand pounds over the course of their confinement. And where does all that meat come from? To find that out it's best to turn to Deb Guernsey, one of the long-term volunteers of the wolf project who happens to be here today lending her sweat to the building of the Blacktail pen. Deb is thirty-eight, a music school graduate turned dedicated student of, and advocate for, things wild. It was in the spring of this year, when Yellowstone's new arrivals were locked in their traveling crates, prisoners of a court injunction that wouldn't allow them even to be released into their acclimation pens, that Deb decided it was time to do something for wolves. The next day she got on the phone and just like that was working for the Greater Yellowstone Coalition; two months later, thanks in large part to what might best be called her passionate persistence, she landed as a volunteer for the wolf project.

Among her many jobs it would fall to Deb, and later also to a dedicated young woman fresh out of college in Indiana, Carrie Schaefer, to gather what are often not-so-fresh road-killed animals, drive them back to Mammoth and gut them, quarter them when necessary, then haul them into a walk-in cooler where they're stored until needed by the wolves. "It sounds weird," says Deb, "but this was a personal challenge for me, something I'd never done before. The first time I gutted one of those elk I ran into Doug's office all excited, grinning like a ten year old." By late fall Deb and Carrie will be known as "The Carcass Queens." Beyond the obvious grunt work, though, the connections these women have to nurture in order to meet the demand for meat is in itself a piece of management—a tangled web of who's got what that at times seems only slightly less complicated than trying to run an organ donor service with a Rolodex and a telephone. Calls coming in the early hours, telling of a dead elk on U.S. Highway 191 at mile marker 111. Frequent messages from Russ, at the Montana Department of Transportation in Big Sky, who will himself prove so good at the actual stockpiling of carcasses that he must be a shoe-in for "King of the Road Kills."

And thus it is that all manner of strange aspects of the wolf program are revealed under these Douglas-fir, between the pounding of posts and twisting of ratchets in the chill of morning and the near swelter of mid afternoon, first at Blacktail and then at Nez Perce. And at the end of the job we all stand back and look at these fortresses of chain link, which by all rights should be ugly as sin but for a fleeting moment seem almost attractive, if only for their having brought us together. But then again right now I'm blissfully ignorant, clueless about the fever that wolves will soon be throwing against these walls.

EIGHT

What a strange life it's been for the little ones, the pups of wolves Nine and Ten born outside Red Lodge. The first two weeks huddled under a spruce tree with no father, after which comes an urgent middle-of-the-night carry by the scruff of the neck to a new home in a jumble of rocks, the whole time carcasses appearing seemingly out of nowhere, as if dropped from the sky. Then plucked up by a pack of determined humans and not eaten, but tossed into the knotted legs of a pair of coveralls, loaded into a helicopter and hurtled through the air some fifty miles over a massive mountain range, safely grounded, slipped into backpacks and carried by still more humans into a half-acre pen in some remote place God knows where. Thankfully, the early weeks of summer pass quietly for the pups in their quarters at the Rose Creek acclimation pen. Even the manmade dens aren't bad. Given that only the Gray Ghost from the Crystal pack ever used those hulking plywood security boxes placed throughout each pen site, the recovery team has given Nine and her pups something decidedly more appealing. Architecturally the new digs could be described as classic hovel—small triangular structures made out of logs with flat roofs covered first with tarps and then piled with spruce branches. On the day the nine wolves were flown back to Yellowstone, the recovery team carefully placed the eight pups inside one of these rustic mock dens, at which point mom promptly went in and carted every last one of them off to the other. There they stayed for a good month or so, rarely even poking their heads out when the two-leggeds came around three times a week, offering food and checking water.

It takes until about the third week in June, about weaning time, for the pups to start really finding their legs. Now when workers come in, instead of hiding out in the mock den a few dash off into the security boxes, while others follow that ancient and wise mammal maxim that says when in doubt, do exactly as mom does. Or at least take a good stab at it. And mom, just as she did last winter during her first round of confinement in this pen, paced the fence. And then paced it some more. During feedings these days, the recovery team spots three or four or five pups doing their best to tag along with her in the far corner of the pen, several steps behind, stumbling around and bumping into one another but more or less managing to move one way along the chain link, turn around, and then twitter and steamroll back again, the size of their legs demanding ten steps for every one of hers. One day Mark Johnson watches Nine trot over a log without giving it a thought, while the black pup close behind her runs up to it, leaps with all his might, smacks into the top of the log, and falls over on his back. That happy, clumsy stage, when life is nothing if not a contact sport.

It's about this time when one of the seven black pups treats Doug Smith to a stirring blast from the past. As you may recall, the father of these youngsters, big number Ten, was the only animal of the fourteen original Yellowstone wolves that instead of pacing nervously in the far corner of his acclimation pen at the approach of humans would instead run a more circular route, actually venturing behind the recovery team workers, even loping past the dreaded pen door that every other animal recoiled from. Oh, there were one or two other wolves that would on rare occasion lap the pen. But for them it was the exception. For Ten it was routine. "I go in to feed one day," Smith says soberly, sounding moved by the experience, "and all of a sudden one of these little pups—just one of them— heads out, real clumsy like, and runs this big circle around me, exactly as his father did. I don't know. Having fed that big male some twenty times and then seeing his pup doing exactly the same thing, man, it was exciting."

The pups are vaccinated on June 26th, at two months; all in all they're in excellent condition, weighing in at an average of about eighteen pounds. By now they have the facial features of honest-to-goodness wolves. Their mouths and sharp teeth have been growing especially fast, and seem every bit as out of proportion to the size of their bodies as their big feet. While at the time of capture in Red Lodge seven of the pups were uniformly black, since then they've acquired patches of gray over each shoulder that wrap up and around to meet at the middle of their upper backs. As for the lone gray pup, while she won't wear the beautiful light-colored coat of her father, number Ten, the tinges of reddish brown in her fur bear a strong resemblance to that wonderful lone wolf, number Seven. It's worth noting that besides mouths and teeth and colored coats, these pups have also acquired a real attitude against being caught. On vaccination day they hide from veterinarian Mark Johnson for dear life inside the manmade dens, fully half of them somehow plastering themselves into a tiny nook formed by the overlap of two logs.

All in all, everything seems to be going swimmingly. Of course where wolves are concerned, the only thing you can count on is that there is very little you can really count on. Do what you will, but nothing stays neat and tidy for long. On July 29th, on a dark night wrapped in a froth of clouds, an enormous wind comes roaring out of the west across the northern tier of the park, screaming across the Buffalo Plateau and down Slough Creek, running crazy across the hills behind the Buffalo Ranch, down the gully and through the spruce grove that holds the Rose Creek acclimation pen with its eight pups and mother wolf. Now as either fate or the wolves would have it, six trees go down that night, two of them, big Englemann spruce, falling at different locations on top of the fence. Again, the acclimation pens are constructed out of long runs of steel panels, ten foot by ten foot, each one joined to the next with three butter-fly-shaped stainless steel clamps; the falling trees pop the clamps off and crush two panels in different parts of the pen, more or less dou-bling them over on themselves. At one site under the fallen tree is a small hole in the link. And as luck would have it, it's just about the right size to allow free passage by a twelve-week-old wolf pup.

And so it is that two days later the recovery team loads their packs and sets off on the half-mile-long trail up the gully, expecting another routine day at the office, only to find mom doing her pac-ing thing in the far corner of the pen, and not a pup in sight. Vanished. Up and gone. After the initial shock wears off—and mind you, this is one hell of a shock—heads go together, chins are rubbed, and finally the team settles on a plan, at least for the short term. They reason that Nine isn't likely to bolt out behind the pups through that tight little hole, especially given how reluctant she was back in March to walk through far bigger openings. On the other hand, as much fun as all this running around must be for the kids, there'll soon come a time when what they'll want most is to be back with mom. The plan, then, is to hike back up at daybreak, assume that at least some of the pups will have moved back inside, then wire the hole shut. From all appearances the other damaged panel was crushed in such a way that it doesn't seem like a wolf can use it as a passage out; for the time being it's left as is.

At the crack of dawn the team is back again, and sure enough, there are two pups in the pen. Hardly a great catch, but better than nothing. Two down and six to go. The entry hole is closed off and further plans are made to try a kennel trap—one of those inventions almost kid-like in its simplicity, where you tie a hunk of meat with a string at the back of the cage and then run the string to a stick in the door. Much to their surprise, the next day the team comes back to find not two pups inside the pen but three. Hmmm. Now how did that happen? On closer examination it appears that one of the pups has managed to climb up the fallen tree still lying against the second panel, then jump the three or so feet down into the pen. Soon afterward the kennel trap gets another one, and that makes four. Over the next five days no one gets out, leaving the team to conclude that while the fallen tree on the second panel may let a wolf come in by walking up the trunk and then bailing off into the pen, as one pup apparently already did, it doesn't let them back out again. Perfect. A one-way door.

The kennel trap doesn't seem to be fooling anyone else, so the team moves to the next level of their arsenal, the padded leghold with a trap transmitter, which means round-the-clock monitoring so that as soon as the device trips the animal can be secured and replaced in the pen. At the same time an effort is launched to find a good observation point on either side of the gully from which the team can watch the pups without them knowing it. Eventually the men find a good spot over on the east ridge, though not before Doug Smith, Mike Phillips, and tracker Carter Neimeyer walk up on a grizzly bear sitting in the grass on the west ridge, stuffing himself full of yampa. The good news is that the bear acts like he could care less, and Neimeyer ends up getting some video footage that most tourists would sell their kids for. Needless to say, that encoun-

103

ter, less than a quarter mile from the pen, adds a certain pique to subsequent nighttime treks to and from the pen—especially considering the area around the site is now scattered with traps containing baits and scents that bears are likely to find enticing. Walking into this area after dark the boys seem committed to stopping on the ridge lines and scanning with those big flashlights of theirs with the fresh batteries, sweeping in both directions and then down the other side, in what from a distance must look like floodlights on a used car lot at a midnight madness sale.

It isn't exactly that the leghold traps don't work. In fact one black pup is caught right away on the first night, promptly popped back into the pen, raising the number to five. The following day, much to everyone's horror, there's an extra black pup out again, though it's impossible to say whether it was the one just caught. The next night two more are caught and replaced in the pen, including the one gray pup of the litter, and another one trips the trap but pulls his leg out and gets away. The following morning two have escaped yet again, including the gray.

This is the wedge of that summer of 1995 that Doug Smith describes as a dark day. A major crisis. The pups got out, and what's worse, they've been given valuable lessons about the dangers of traps. From the team's observation point on the east ridge it fast becomes apparent just how much the pups have learned. The young wolves have been spending most of their time hanging out about a quarter mile north of the pen, on a quiet hillside with tall grass and a fine stand of old aspen. Then, every evening around dusk, they work their way back to the pen to fraternize, to catch up on things with mom and siblings. But after springing the traps their route down to the pen becomes amazingly convoluted. They know full well that traps are set to the north, and so they give that entire area a wide berth, coming up instead from a point well to the south. "There's this one night," recalls Smith, "we're watching as they approach a trap. Now this thing is extremely well hidden, well disguised. But they notice it, and when they do they immediately jump off to the side."

It's probably not much consolation, but if the wolf catching isn't so good, at least the wolf watching is. The pups are going after mice, trapping them against the ground with their front paws, playing with one another in the tall grass, and in one case having a fairly dramatic encounter with a pair of coyotes. "Three of the pups were hanging out at that little spot they liked so much," Doug recalls. "Up there in the aspen. We weren't sure where the fourth one was. Anyway, from our high spot we see these two coyotes making a straight line for them. They know right where those pups are and they're moving in. I say to Mike 'This is it. We're going to see a pup get killed.' The very thing we'd been worrying about, and now it was going to happen right in front of us." The pups are quick to get a whiff of the trouble coming, and one of them bids a hasty farewell to his kin and makes a mad dash straight for some heavy cover in the spruce. The other two, though, position themselves on an old rotted log and stand their ground. "It almost seemed like the coyotes weren't sure what they'd stumbled across. They hesitated. And then these two little pups actually made a move toward the coyotes. And they backed off. I don't know if you could say the pups exactly chased them off, but they sure moved them away. And that was the end of it."

When it's all said and done the team manages to catch five of the eight pups. They fix the fence for real, decide that everyone who's gettable has been gotten, pull out the trapping equipment, and head for home. All they can do now is keep delivering carcasses and rounds of good wishes to the little adventurers still running around outside the pen. It's interesting to note that while grizzlies have been common in this area, coming as close as a quarter mile from the pen, none have come up to the fence line to investigate the meat that's being left, though surely they can smell it. Some biologists have maintained for years that adult grizzlies and wolves seem to have a level of mutual respect for one another when it comes to certain acts of trespass; even if that's true, it's amazing to think that those manners might apply even to wolves locked away in a pen. Throughout all this turmoil, this long string of sleepless nights, I hear fresh rounds of curses against Chad McKittrick. When you haven't slept for days, when you're buckling under the enormous labor and expense required to baby-sit nine wolves three times a week in the heat of summer—let alone trap and replace eight escapees—it's hard to not think of the fact that none of this would have been necessary had Ten not taken Chad's bullet on that hill above Scotch Coulee.

Back in the other world the critics are back out in force, singing forte, going on about how the Park Service is being too heavy handed, that they're keeping the pups in the pen too long. Overmanaging again. They should just let nature take its course. But the fact is that over the course of the summer it's become increasingly clear that political pressures are such that there will at best be one more round of wolves coming into Yellowstone from Canada, and at this particular moment in time there's some question as to whether even that will happen. Either way, every wolf in this ecosystem has taken on incredible significance.

There's no arguing that if the recovery team can hold the pups until after hunting season—that time of year when there's by far the largest number of humans roaming the surrounding wild lands—they'll greatly minimize the chance of these wolves encountering people. It isn't so much that hunters will shoot them, though certainly that could happen. It's more that if you release these wolves before they've any shred of territorial footing, and they leave the park and end up getting pushed back and forth by running into a lot of people, that could be enough to make them start ranging farther than they would if allowed to settle in at a time of relative quiet. Clearly, holding wolves in the pen isn't a good thing. But it's the conservative approach, the course of action most likely to protect the animals, not to mention the millions of dollars already invested in this reintroduction program.

By September the politics of the pups has grown heavy and stale, like subway air. What's more, the lunacy at home is growing, Chad continuing to play man-turns-myth, and letters to the editor warning about how wolves will soon be nabbing our children and generally causing the end of life as we know it. All in all it seems like a good time to hit the backcountry, maybe go see what the Crystal pack finds so enticing about life in the wilds of Pelican Creek.

*   *   *   *   *

Yellowstone spins some of its best magic not on the tops of mountains or in the dark cracks of its canyons, but in the easy tumble of its valleys. In mile after mile of bison-tramped meadows stitched with Timothy and fescue, yampa and sage, green in early summer then gold through fall, the edge of every grassy sweep cradled by timber-covered hills. Places like Lamar and Slough Creek and The Thoroughfare. And in the very heart of the park, the beautiful Pelican Valley. It's coming on mid-September, more than two weeks past the hard frosts that puckered the heads of the yampa and biscuit root, nudged the mats of huckleberry and geranium leaves from green to crimson. In the shade of the trees are still a few scattered patches of lupine, worn-out purple tossed into the deep shadows of the spruce, along with smatters of aster, salsify, and harebell. For all the moisture early in the season the faucet has been dry for an awfully long time now, and dust kicks from our heels with every step. The yampa is looking especially puny this year, dessicated, which along with a sorry crop of pine nuts would seem to bode poorly for the region's grizzlies. Up ahead an osprey preens on a lodgepole snag and then launches with a gentle hop to pluck a trout from Pelican Creek, easy, showing about as much effort as the rest of us might use to grab a gum wrapper blowing half-speed across the lawn. Raptors trace circles in the sky, as blue as a sky can be.

My wife Jane and I, along with a good friend from Red Lodge, are quietly tramping up the lower reaches of the valley, pulled up this long, gentle slope as if by some invisible hand, enchanted in much the way that in sleep dreams can pull you back and forth between the known and the fancied. All around are the sounds of groaning bison and the fluted yodel of sandhill cranes, the croak of ravens and the occasional elk bugle breaking out of the forest. Well ahead, on the north side of the valley, a gray plume from a small thermal feature erupts now and then, steamy sighs breaking free of earth and hovering for a time as gray puffs in the still, hot air. Having been thoroughly wired with the world when I tossed on the backpack around ten this morning, by lunch I find it hard to be concerned with anything at all. Life has gone back to wordless rhythms, to the patient, relentless comings and goings of things wild.

The crows and bluebirds and warblers are beginning to flock, and when we look skyward to the southwest toward Yellowstone Lake, as often as not there are V-shaped lines of Canada geese. Red-tails too can be seen hanging in the air, but as for one of my favorite raptors, the Swainson's hawks, they're nowhere to be seen; most likely they've quit Yellowstone for another year and are already heading south, opting to spend winter someplace warm, like Argentina. Gone too are the prairie falcons and hummingbirds, the latter pushed out by the dwindling collection of wildflowers. It's this going away of things that leaves me feeling melancholy, that shreds the splendid illusion I cast way back in the prime of summer, when it seemed *109* endings of any kind were a rumor that would never come to pass.

As of late the Crystal pack has been dancing back and forth between Flint and Astringent creeks, trotting now and then past the hissing steam vents and gurgling mud cauldrons that line the oxbows and meanders of upper Pelican. They run the elk, make the occasional kill, and all the while the sub-adults continue to play, chasing one another in the tall grass and romping through the burned woods of the Mirror Plateau. Thinking we might get lucky and catch sight of them, each day at dawn and again at dusk we hike out to the balcony seats on a ridge near Raven Creek, atop a small knoll offering mile-long views down the valley. And each time like clockwork, out from the woods into this weak light come the elk, slowly at first, here a few cows and there a lone bull, building over a half-hour or so until their numbers are in the hundreds, wave after wave drifting across the outer edges of the flats. Cows huddle together, a couple dozen here and there, nabbing mouthfuls of fescue and cinquefoil, while the biggest of the bulls saunter along nearby, pulled by the flush of the rut, for the most part eating nothing at all. The biggest bulls that do find challengers engage them and then run them off, almost casually, like swordsmen stretching, testing, warming up for some bigger battle yet to come; indeed, at this point we're only a week from what will likely be the height of the breeding season. The sparring between larger males is clipped, and yet vigorous enough that we can easily hear the crack of antlers ringing through a mile or more of cold mountain air. And the sharp whistling of their bugling is everywhere—ahead, behind, and to either side of us, outvoicing the grunt of the bison and the chortle of the cranes until it seems all the elk in Yellowstone must be standing in these woods and meadows. Little wonder there would be wolves.

Unknown to us, five of the six wolves of Crystal pack are ten miles to the north across the Mirror Plateau, hunting near Flint Creek, while the remaining animal, a gray sub-adult, number Eight, is by himself in the forest less than a mile away. And that is how it becomes our great fortune to be awoken at dawn the next morning by the main pack coming south again to within a half-mile of us, linking back with Eight through an exchange of long, soulful, four- and five-part howls. I realize that people going on about the effect of hearing wolves howling in the wilderness is one of those subjects so over-talked about and generally run into the ground as to be little but a cliché. And yet when it comes to wake-up calls, suffice it to say I've never felt anything like it.

Part of the buzz, of course, is the grin that comes simply from knowing that here's a sound—ripped from this place well over sixty years ago—now finally back; that alone would tend to give every performance the feel of a celebration. But from a musical point of view, from matters of texture and tonation, such howls frankly seem off the scale. Kind of like the Greek god Pan decided to carry those famous reed pipes of his down to Memphis, and came back to the wilderness a believer in the blues. They're sounds that empty my head of every distraction, that create these big sprawling empty spaces between the rocks and the trees and the clouds in the sky. Apparently wolves relish certain howling events, especially group howlings. Some researchers have noted that at the start of such songfests individual animals will run a considerable distance to join in. All of which makes me think that, while howling certainly serves a practical function, allowing communication between animals and packs across considerable distances, maybe it's also just a lot of fun. As for me, I'd gladly walk fifty miles into the wilds for the chance to be brought back into the morning this way again.

NINE

The week of October 9th, and the decision comes at last to release Nine and her pups to resume their lives in the wild. On the day the team goes in for final processing there's yet another piece of confoundment waiting for them. Instead of five young wolves in the pen, which has been the assumption for months, there are six. Ponder this as you will, there are really only two explanations. The first is that, way back when, workers simply miscounted—entirely possible, of course, but still a bit of stretch. And yet the only other possibility is that somehow a pup managed to get in all by himself. Clearly, the two-foot apron of chain link around the inside edge of the pen would make tunneling in impossible. Which leaves only one other possibility, which if true, seems like wolf magic all over again. In this scenario the pup would have climbed up a ten-foot panel of chain link on the side of the isolation area, basically sticking his paws between the holes in the fence and drawing himself upward, finally reaching the flat roof portion of that holding area, and then leaping off the far side into the interior of the pen.

At this stage the pups are hardly pups anymore. Each has a full

112

complement of permanent teeth, and most weigh in at around sixty-five pounds. And while that's not overly large given their age, it's likely enough wolf to make any roving band of hungry coyotes, maybe even grizzlies, reluctant to mess with them. "There I was earlier this spring at Red Lodge," says Doug Smith, "being shoved up into that rock crevice, taking these tiny pups and throwing them into a net and hauling them out. Then feeding them all summer long. And now here they are these beautiful, hulking animals." It's interesting to note that, despite some people's dire predictions that the earlier handling of these pups in Red Lodge would habituate them to people, there's no sign of that at all. During processing they react with every bit as much terror as any other wild wolf, reinforcing the fact that young will in general take their cues on how to respond to various circumstances from watching the adults in the pack. "When they were very little," Smith says, "they didn't like us at all, though there seemed to be some uncertainty to their reactions, like they weren't entirely sure how to behave. Over time, though, they learned from mom exactly what to do when we were around; by the end we had eight pups acting all alike. She reinforced the notion that these are people, and they're bad. You want to stay away—run up and down the fence on the far side of the pen, duck around the back side. Basically avoid them at all costs."

That kind of caution can make for some tough going when it comes time to catch these pups for final processing. The team decides to use a method Mike Phillips refined when working with red wolves in North Carolina, which involves, of all things, a salmon net—about five feet in diameter, with a five-foot handle. Working in pairs, each person with a net, the workers stand just far enough away from the chain link that the pups will run past them along the fence; with careful timing the net is swung down in front of the pup as it runs by, causing it to take a gentle tumble before coming to rest under the mesh. The handler quietly steps on the net to secure it, while the second handler places his net over the pup as well. The little wolf is carefully untangled, his movements controlled by hold- *113* ing onto the scruff behind each ear, then placed inside one of the large security boxes. (These security boxes, by the way, with removable roofs and lockable doors, are the same ones that the Gray Ghost—the so called "blue wolf" from the Soda Butte group—would hide in at every approach of humans.) At that point additional helpers enter the pen, the roof is lifted, and the pups are all given an injection with a syringe pole that puts them to sleep, allowing them to be weighed, vaccinated, and radio collared without any additional stress.

Speaking of radio collars, from a research standpoint it's significant that these pups are finally big enough to wear collars with three-year batteries, which will give scientists something they never counted on when the project began—a chance for close-up study of the second generation of the Yellowstone wolves. (Of course not all of the pups will end up wearing those collars; the two little mavericks that have continued to roam at large, visiting the family every evening after dark, will escape any handling at all.) One thing these pups are definitely not big or learned enough for, though, is helping mom make kills. Nine is still very much a struggling single mother, in a species that has evolved to channel so many aspects of survival into cooperative family effort.

Then on Wednesday, October 11th, the day of the actual release, one of those wonderful things happens that leaves even the biologists grinning ear to ear, an event that dangles somewhere between the realm of incredible luck and pure wolf wizardry. Filmmaker Ray Paunovich and Collin Phillips are hanging out near the Buffalo Ranch when, to their utter amazement, they happen to see the two pups that have been running free since the fence collapsed in the company of a collared gray adult—tails between their legs, romping with it and rolling on their backs, nipping at its mouth as pups do to gain a meal; the encounter has such a strong air of familiarity to it that some will wonder whether such meetings have happened before. At first everyone assumes this adult is Nine's yearling daughter, Seven, who was herself a former captive at the Rose Creek pen. Such a reunion would be a tremendous stroke of good fortune. The presence of another adult, after all, would go a long, long way in securing care and protection of eight kids—not only as an extra set of eyes and teeth to keep the pups safe from predators, but also to minimize the chance of conflicts with other packs. When Mike Phillips hears about this he grabs a receiver and rushes out to listen for the signal from her collar, finds it isn't Seven at all. In scanning for signals from other wolves Phillips discovers it's someone even better—one of the young bachelors from the Crystal Pack, number Eight. At a time of the year when wolves are generally coalescing, starting to become more cohesive for the winter ahead, Eight has over the past three weeks been engaged in all manner of solo jaunts; in fact the last time he was located by radio telemetry, a week ago, he was running around well to the southwest, near the Grand Canyon of the Yellowstone. By no small miracle he's chosen to come courting just before his potential partner is due to gain her freedom. A match made in heaven. She gets a caregiver. He gets a fat promotion in his social status, from underling to alpha male. Maybe it's a case of growing to fit the shoes, but this is the beginning of a remarkable transition for a wolf that in the pen seemed small, with a mediocre coat, one who routinely cowered in the presence of the alpha male. In the coming weeks he'll appear more in charge, stronger; even his coat will seem more vibrant and full.

Having learned from their efforts last spring, on release day the recovery team goes in and removes an entire fence panel from the pen; again, they do this near the wolves' comfort zone, since these animals have always shown a strong aversion to going anywhere near the gate used by humans. Once again a remote camera is set up just outside the new exit in hopes of getting photos of the big walk to freedom. And what do the wolves do? They depart by way of the gate, leaving the camera to click off a bunch of photos of flapping ravens. After their departure a grizzly bear is seen walking around the pen area, back and forth through the panel, no doubt checking out the carcasses. By eleven o'clock that morning, all ten wolves are spotted together, on a snow-covered hill a mile or so east of Rose Creek.

A week after Nine and her pups are released, one of the most remarkable behavioral events of the year happens in the west end of the valley—a flash from wolf college that leaves Mike Phillips and filmmakers Bob Landis and Ray Paunovich shaking their heads in disbelief. All ten members of the Rose Creek group (which now includes number Eight, formerly from Crystal), are hanging out on a bench in the west end of the Lamar Valley, near Lamar Canyon, feeding on a bison—the carcass of an animal that died accidentally during a brucelosis research project. The Crystal pack, meanwhile, is in the same general area, at this point still unaware of the Rose Creek group, but heading west, right for them. On making visual contact the alpha pair of Crystal, numbers Four and Five, make a quick 180-degree turn and run off back to the east, while the three sub-adults keep loping in the direction of the Rose Creek wolves. Meanwhile, the alpha female of Rose Creek, number Nine, is waiting down the hill, somewhat apart from the group, acting very nervous, agitated by what she sees, barking. The three Crystal wolves keep closing the gap, though, finally ending up face to face with their brother, number Eight, along with the crew of pups he's just adopted. The pups sit and watch as Eight moves over to give a big wolf howdy to his brothers, and in the process evidently decide these guys must be okay, because step-dad says so. Before you know it twelve wolves are romping and bouncing around, having a grand old time. Two of the Crystal yearlings, though, are quick to sense the agitation coming from the Rose Creek alpha female, and decide the reunion is officially over, one departing east, one west; Six, though, is still enjoying himself, and so together he and his brother, Eight, start walking down the hill toward number Nine.

Wolf number Eight, who's after all new to this whole business of being an alpha male, has made a terrible mistake. Sort of the equivalent of some guy deciding to celebrate his wedding night by running off with his old college buddies to down a few drinks at the corner tap. His new mate, Rose Creek alpha Nine, is not pleased. Not at all. She continues barking loudly, then advances toward this happy-go-lucky brother-in-law. It isn't until Nine gets in his face and starts being seriously aggressive that Six finally catches on, at which point Eight gets the message, too: Nine clearly does not want any strangers hanging around her pups. In that split second of understanding he turns on his brother, and together he and Nine take off after him. The three wolves careen down the hillside, with Six caught smack in the middle between Nine and Eight—suddenly a very dangerous place to be. Out of the tumble and skirmish that ensues comes a line of wolves flying east across the meadows, Six in the lead. Pretty soon Nine backs off, but Eight, maybe trying to convince his partner that yes, I really do get it, keeps up this high-speed chase of his brother, slowly gaining on him, running him hard for nearly four hundred yards before finally peeling off.

One of the other two Crystal sub-adults has rejoined the alpha pair, but the other—the one who scampered west—now finds himself out by his lonesome, wanting desperately to get back to his group but separated by that crazy brother of his and his new mate. He starts howling, and pretty soon his pack howls back. Moving with great caution, giving the Rose Creek animals a wide berth, the black sub-adult works his way south and then east, finally manages to rejoin his group. As for the Rose Creek pair and the pups, they regroup at the place where they first encountered number Six, and soon everyone in that family is playing and prancing together and having the finest of times.

Up until this moment, some members of the recovery team wondered whether the alphas or even the sub-adults from another pack might be aggressive toward the pups; these smaller, less-experienced wolves, after all, wouldn't likely be very good at protecting themselves. And who knows, that might have been exactly what would have happened had Eight—a sibling to those Crystal sub-adults—not been there to make that initial contact such a friendly one. So much learning going on in such a short amount of time! Biologists learned that, yes, the Rose Creek pack can take care of itself and then some, a realization that's sending sighs of relief down the valley big enough to rustle the branches of the Douglas-fir. What's more, it was fascinating to see that the alphas of both packs wanted nothing to do with this encounter. It was the younger animals that initiated the interaction; even Nine didn't really get involved until the very end.

Exactly why that is, it's hard to say. The truth is such encounters are rarely seen, and it takes an awful lot of eye-witnessing to formulate any reliable theories about what's going on in the world of wolves. But no reason we can't do a little speculating. For one thing, the Crystal alpha pair probably has had enough experience to know that running into other wolves is almost never a good thing; such meetings often result in serious conflicts, and when the teeth start flying more often than not they're aimed at the alpha pair. Also, territories aren't yet firmly established here in Yellowstone, so it's

118

hardly likely this pair would feel justified in making a vigorous defense over this particular patch of ground. And finally, if you're part of a breeding alpha pair, your position in the pack is already firmly anchored. There's no real value in checking out other wolves, the way there would be for single sub-adults, who may be looking for mates. In this case, the natural inclination of the Crystal sub-adults to investigate other wolves is furthered by the fact that the group they're encountering offers absolutely no threatening signals; the yearlings know their brother number Eight, after all, and the pups are acting as pups always do in the presence of strange adult wolves—thoroughly submissive, ears laid back, tails between their legs, mouth open. What's the harm in checking it out?

As for the pups, this was almost certainly their first encounter with other wolves. Initially they may have gone into this thinking, "Great! Friends of Dad's means more wolves to play with!" But by watching their mother's severe reaction against Six, ending with both her and her new mate chasing him up the valley like bouncers after a bar thug, the kids likely walked away knowing they just can't be friendly with every wolf they happen to stumble across. And finally, thanks to a few stern words and some ear twisting by his new mate, Eight probably now has it firmly in mind that he's the alpha male of his own pack now, step-father to eight young ones. As such, it's no longer okay to play back-slap with the wolves of another pack, even if they are his own brothers.

And with that the two groups part company, Crystal making for the Mirror Plateau, Rose Creek splitting in two, half the group moving toward the Rose Creek pen, the other half to Specimen Ridge, where they continue to feed on that bison carcass. As for Soda Butte, who witnessed none of this, they're neck deep in peace and quiet well to the north, in those sweet, golden meadows above the Slough Creek cabin.

* * * * *

At the same time the Rose Creek pups are finally getting their first taste of life in the wild, the man who killed their father and sent them into an acclimation pen for four-and-a-half months is on trial in Billings. After jury selection, which includes such probing questions from defense attorney Gil Burdett as "Is there anyone here who believes everything they read in the paper?" opening statements begin after lunch on October 23rd. Burdett tells the jury he'll be focusing on the fact that there's a historic problem of dogs running loose in Red Lodge (quite correct), and further, that the Park Service wasn't being forthright about where the wolves were located (in truth, they were being so forthright around the time of this killing that even some members of the media were suggesting they clam up a bit, that someone who wanted to do the animals harm would know right where to find them). In characterizing the events following the actual shooting, Burdett admits right off that "things got stupid, to say the least." From all appearances the jury seems a typical cross section of Montanans. And yet Chad doesn't look at all comfortable in front of them; his face is flushed, and his leg bounces for the entire afternoon, like it's gone into some kind of spasm. Then again maybe some of that has to do with sitting ten feet from prosecutor Ed Laws—a broad-shouldered, no-nonsense man with a strong, angular face; intelligent, calculating—not exactly the kind of guy most people would relish going up against.

Dusty Steinmasel is the old friend of Chad's who was along for this entire debacle, and is now serving as chief witness for the prosecution. When he first takes the stand he makes eye contact one time with Chad, blanches at the look he gets back, and never once glances at him again. In a thoroughly muddled recounting of the conversation that took place on first sighting the animal, he says there was definitely discussion with Chad about whether or not this was a wolf. Later, after the shooting, Steinmasel says he followed Chad the 140 yards up the hill, all the while feeling in his gut that Chad had nailed somebody's pet. Once on top, of course, they found out otherwise. "Chad," Dusty says he told him, seeming to relive the sense of panic he was feeling at the time, "this is a big fucking deal." Dusty goes on to say he told Chad that, if he wasn't going to report what happened, then he needed to get him out of there. Shortly afterward, though, the two men headed to Belfry for gas and a twelve pack of beer—thinking medicine, I guess—after which Chad decided he was going back to get that wolf, that right or wrong the thing was his now, and that he wasn't going to just leave it sitting there on that hill. And in the end Dusty went along, helping drag the wolf down the hill to the truck, even going so far as to lend a hand skinning out the carcass. "Here we were sitting by the side of the road with this million-dollar wolf," Steinmasel says. "It was going to take forever to skin it. I figured I might as well help and get it over with."

When agent Tim Eiker later came to Steinmasel's house on April 27th asking if he'd seen anything out of the ordinary on the road above his house, Dusty said no. (Oddly, Eiker actually knew Steinmasel and his ex-wife from a time when all three were living in New Mexico; they weren't exactly friends, Eiker said, but they were friendly.) The following Wednesday Eiker returned, asking specifically about Chad McKittrick. By that time Dusty had been sweating bullets over the whole incident. "I wasn't eating," he tells the court. "Wasn't sleeping. Looking up and down the road every time a car went by." Clearly he wasn't as good as Chad when it came to blotting out negative thoughts. According to Dusty, two weeks after the shooting he had a conversation with his friend, during which Chad apologized for getting him involved. "I've been sitting here drunk for two weeks," Chad supposedly told him, "while you've been running around paranoid."

By the following Saturday that paranoia got to be too much, and Dusty cracked. He placed a call to Eiker's phone machine and left a message that he had a tale to tell, though on first telling it included no mention of the part he played in the crime. "I thought Chad would take responsibility for his actions and leave me out," as the two had previously agreed.

121

When the agents finally showed up at Chad MicKittrick's house with a search warrant, he was expecting them. Chad will testify this week that he'd talked with Dusty after agent Eiker first started coming around asking questions; that the two even discussed the reward money of $13,000 offered by various wildlife organizations—how Dusty said he could retire off that. Way back in May, when I saw Chad on the ranch at Willow Creek, I too asked him about the reward money, telling him I was surprised Dusty hadn't offered half the money in exchange for turning him in. "Oh, he did," Chad said matter of factly. After telling the agents where the hide and head were located, Chad and Tim Eiker sat around the kitchen table for thirty minutes or so, Chad alternately in good spirits, then breaking into tears, often referring to the dead wolf as "Aurora"—the name he'd seen on Ten's collar, chosen and carefully lettered with brightly colored markers by school children from Hinton, Alberta. Chad even showed Eiker a prized postcard he'd collected of a wolf. "Did you understand the defendant to express an affinity for wolves?" the defense attorney asks Eiker.

"Yes."

Over the objections of the defense, photos are passed around of the dead wolf to the jury, and a couple of the jurors wrinkle their noses at the sight. The bullet, explains pathologist Richard Stroud, passed completely through the animal, "destroying both liver and lung tissue, causing death rather rapidly."

Then comes a long parade of witnesses: forensics and genetics experts from Oregon verifying that yes, this is in fact number Ten; a Red Lodge rancher testifying as to the dangers of wolves and dogs to local livestock; even the manager of the Sunlight Basin ranch, where the wolf was killed, saying that no, there was no livestock on the property at the time—at least not any there legally—and that even if there was any, Chad had no authority to control predators there. When Chad finally takes the stand, he recounts the same basic story as Dusty, though in his version, unlike Dusty's, there was never any verbal acknowledgment that the animal might have been a wolf before it was shot. I recall a point during the summer when Chad stopped referring to the animal as a wolf altogether, often catching himself in mid sentence, quickly replacing the word with "wild dog." Almost like he was being coached into a new way of talking. "When I shot that wild dog," he'd say, emphasizing the wild dog part. Listening to his testimony today, that affectation still lingers.

In truth a great deal of what comes up in the trial seems super-fluous, considering that it doesn't matter a whit whether Chad knew he was shooting a wolf or not. While there are provisions in the Endangered Species Act for accidental killings, they're designed for people like trappers who catch an endangered animal on a trap line, or someone hitting one with a car. When it comes to guns, there does seem to be that small, but in the West sometimes revolution-ary, concept that people are supposed to know what they're shooting. And yet in the end the "Chad didn't know" approach is about the only straw the defense can cling to. "Does it make sense?" defense attorney Gil Burdett asks in his closing arguments. "Is it realistic? Does someone jump out (of his truck) and cause himself that much trouble?"

The jury deliberates for only a couple of hours, and finds Chad guilty on all counts.

TEN

After a month of mostly dry weather, snow has been falling around Red Lodge for three days, winter confetti, saved up by the heavens to bring in the new year. There are forty and fifty inches of fresh powder in the mountains, two feet outside my door and still coming. Weather not fit for a gaggle of geese to fly in, let alone for airplanes meant to track wolves. Ten o'clock at night on the 2nd of January I get a phone call from a friend, a small-scale rancher living to the north, outside Roberts. "Have you heard the wolves are back?" he says. I haven't. It's the Soda Butte pack again, running like the breath of a Chinook in great, ragged circles: from the wind-blasted canyon of the Stillwater to the Clarks Fork, across the mountains to Red Lodge and the Beartooth Front. Then, when the mood strikes, back over the plateau to Cooke City and Slough Creek, loping some thirty miles through the night with less thought than most of us would muster to drive across town for a movie at the mall. There are any number of wolf traits that people seem to connect to—the play, the look, the howl. But it's the traveling I can't get over. Some nights I lie in bed looking out through the aspen and across the creek toward the place where the moon hovers on the crest of the East Bench, wishing more than anything I could know what it is to run through the night like that, twilight to dawn, enormous paws whispering against the fluff.

124

As usual, there's no end of fear and loathing clipping at their heels. The latest frenzy has erupted over an incident several weeks ago outside the community of Fishtail, when a young hunting dog out with its owner cut tracks from the Soda Butte pack and followed the scent, stumbled onto the wolves, and was killed. Doug Smith had flown two days prior, on Wednesday, December 6th, and located the Soda Butte pack up the Stillwater Canyon, several miles downstream from one of their favorite stomping grounds around Flood Creek. As usual he called in the pack's location both to the state of Montana and U.S. Fish and Wildlife. On the next flight, two days later, Smith failed to pick up signals from any of the Soda Butte animals, and after a lengthy search headed back empty-handed. Unbeknown to anyone at the time, the group had actually moved downstream out of the canyon to a place near Reeves Pond, which is where they ended up killing the hunting dog; the residents of Fishtail were convinced the feds were intentionally keeping the location of those wolves a secret.

And that's when things turned ridiculous. The emotional brush fire sparked by this event likely could have been controlled had U.S. Fish and Wildlife simply visited with locals, or at least made a few well-placed phone calls explaining how they'd lost track of the wolves. But there were no visits, no calls. I get the sense there are some sitting in the command seats of the wolf program who over the years have come to feel thoroughly hung out to dry, who've suffered under verbal threats and assaults for so many years that some days it's hard for them to believe in the worth of talking at all. When your back gets pinned against the wall often enough, it's easy to start flinching at the notion of building bridges and mending fences, easy to start coloring routine communication as some kind of needless exercise in hand holding. Decisions start being driven by paranoia, by personal concerns about how best to stay safe. And while all that may be understandable, it's also unforgivable. When that hunting dog was killed people needed a face, a voice in the same room, even one guy about whom, five years from now, at least a handful of ranchers could say "well, I hate all this wolf crap but at least so-and-so shot straight with us. At least maybe we can trust him." Without that the reactions come bigger, and they come more often. Conspiracy theories begin to smolder, and suddenly the Shoot, Shovel, and Shut-Up Club starts looking like a reasonable alternative even to reasonable men.

Part of the U.S. Fish and Wildlife agency's job is supposed to be to help cultivate more realistic attitudes toward wolves; indeed, over the years Joe Fontaine has given literally hundreds of talks meant to do just that. But attitudes about wolves don't tend to change in the quiet times; they change, either for good or for bad, in the midst of a crisis like this one. Let's face it: if you're a member of the wolf recovery team you can pretty much rule out ever being a regular at Sunday dinners with livestock growers. And yet you can never afford to ignore the fact that the welfare of wolves rests to no small degree in the hands of the locals.

In short, the handling of the Fishtail incident could well serve as a federal training film for how to hang yourself. And yet on the other hand, it's worth noting that any chance the feds have of turning into halfway decent neighbors with ranchers over the long term is being undermined by a far more pervasive force—by that undisputed king of wolf-related ignorance peddling, the master of paranoia politics, U. S. Senator Conrad Burns of Montana. Burns has made it his personal mission for over a year to gut the Fish and Wildlife staff by poisoning the money well. Considering that wolves

126 are already here, the real consequence of that vendetta is to leave the agency increasingly unavailable in those times when ranchers could really use them—when livestock predation actually occurs. At this point just one lone field biologist remains, Joe Fontaine, and he and Ed Bangs are responsible not only for addressing any wolf-related problems that may arise, both in the recovery area of northwest Montana and the experimental area around Yellowstone, but also for collaring packs so they can be monitored in the years to come. This winter Burns warned the Department of the Interior's Mollie Beattie that he'd force even deeper cuts next year, not only in Fish and Wildlife budgets, but in the Park Service, as well. Burns appears to be having the time of his life lording over the demise of a federal project he never liked in the first place, swashing to the crowd like some playground bully after busting the nose of the class nerd. From a sordid political perspective, such antics may play out beautifully. After washing out funding, Burns can point to the lack of proper oversight by Fish and Wildlife in tending to problem wolves, shrug, put his hand on the shoulder of some poor rancher, and say, "Well, Frank, ya know I told them this would happen. Those damn feds." Never mind that as the years pass and wolves increase, it'll be Frank's livestock that end up as ante for the game.

With the Soda Butte group now hanging out just north of Red Lodge, my neighbors from the East Bench and the sage draws of Dry Creek, from Belfry and even Bridger, are whipping up all manner of scary thoughts. Even if the wolves aren't bothering their cattle right now, they tell me, it's only four weeks to calving season. And what then? "I want to know how to stop this wolf thing," one of them tells Animal Damage Control tracker Carter Neimeyer on New Year's night, seething, sounding like a man who honestly does believe that his very life, let alone his livelihood, is hanging by a thread. "You tell me. How do I stop them?"

As it turns out, the Park Service is getting nervous, too. It's been weeks since anyone saw the lone pup born to the Soda Butte pack in the spring, and while any number of things could have happened to it, it's hard not to think he may have gone down by bullet, just like number Ten. Curious pups, after all, have a knack for finding all kinds of ways to get themselves into trouble. Much to the dismay of both sides of the wolf issue, the Soda Butte pack seems determined to push into the heart of ranching country now and then, and there's little to be done about it, short of picking them up and hauling them back to the park every time they stray (a plan actually being pushed by some of the same people who are showering accolades on Conrad Burns for gutting funds for this project). In a meeting in Yellowstone, it's decided that Mike Phillips and Doug Smith—with the blessings of the Fish and Wildlife Service—will head east to Red Lodge, to do some tracking of the Soda Butte pack, but perhaps more importantly, to pull chairs around kitchen tables in a few ranch houses and do a little talking. Nobody's kidding themselves; anything these guys say will be a tough sell. At the first place they visit four ranchers have gathered; the owner greets them at the door, trying to hold back Queenie the dog. "Don't worry," he says. "She's friendly except to people who work for the federal government." At least he's smiling.

The majority of these ranchers are decent, reasonable men. And while you'd be hard pressed to find even a handful who welcome the idea of bringing back wolves, most of them, letters to the editor to the contrary, don't see it as the end of the world. Yet this particular debate is defined by the extremes—moderates leaving the stage to those with a penchant for running around screaming the sky is falling. And with an issue like wolves, unpopular to begin with and thick with uncertainty, any rumor spreads like grass fire in a big wind. Take the case of Bob Kero's cow. On January 1st—the same time wolves were spotted in the Red Lodge-Roberts area—Kero's cattle were spooked by something—just what, he can't and won't say. The only casualty was a heifer who lost the end of her tail. "Whatever it was," he explains, "got only a mouthful of cow hair flavored by the part that goes over the fence last." Two days later, at a public meeting on the wolf reintroduction in Billings with Mike Phillips, one of Kero's neighbors stands up and embellishes the story, sounding like a man going for the course record at a liar's tournament, claiming that seven cows had been maimed by wolves. By the next morning Kero's phone is ringing off the hook—not just from worried neighbors, but from the media, including the Billings NBC affiliate, which calls Kero to ask for an interview to discuss the eight cows he had killed by wolves. Now, Kero is no fan of wolf reintroduction. Yet much to his credit he takes the time to pen a letter to a couple of the local papers, pleading for honesty. "This is the worst thing that could have been done to ranchers," he says of his neighbor's idiotic remarks. "Why would we want to shoot ourselves in the foot?"

By the time Phillips and Smith make it to Roberts, the Soda Butte wolves have left, given up these open ranch lands and are back on the move, heading west. On January 9th, Doug Smith spots five animals near the West Rosebud. At first he assumes they're the original five animals of the group, minus the missing pup; yet curiously, only four of the five are giving off radio signals. There's no signal at all coming from number Twelve, which is the black wolf with the spayed foot. And that means one of two things: Either Twelve's collar is on the fritz, or else, and far more likely, he's broken away from the pack and is off somewhere doing his own thing, in which case the fifth wolf must be the animal no one has seen for weeks and was feared dead—the lone Soda Butte pup.

Among mammals there are those species that tend to grow up fast. Creatures that all but hit the ground running, able to travel and to some extent fend for themselves just days after birth. Snowshoe hares, for example. Or bison calves, which are able to be on their feet just fifteen minutes after birth. These quick starters are known as "precocial" animals, and for them life is far different than for species like primates and homo sapiens and wolves—so-called "atricial" animals—whose offspring spend months and even years being coddled and cooed to and tended on all fronts before they're strong enough to go off on their own. But even within atricial species there are always a few individuals who seem especially bright—we call it precocious—who are off walking, exploring, or in the case of humans, talking, doing math problems, or getting hooked on phonics while their peers are still locked in goo-goo land. The Soda Butte pup may well be one of those. Gifted and talented. A prodigy. If so it would have been easy for him to end up alone the last time the pack blew down the Stillwater heading for Red Lodge, the trip when the hunting dog was killed near Fishtail. Maybe he was off chasing red squirrels or nosing after whitetails or simply seeing what the view looked like from some distant ridge while Mom, Dad, and siblings just loped away, leaving him stuck out there on his own. Meanwhile his family goes off to Red Lodge and Roberts, even stops off for a brief visit to the Red Lodge Mountain Ski Area. (One avid skier tells me later he wishes they'd stay right there on the slopes, nab some of those obnoxious snow boarders.) It's nothing but a guess, but from Red Lodge they may have gone up and over the mountains to the Clark Fork and then back over into the Stillwater; then a short time later reversed that same trip, making the yawning, thirty-some-mile loop counter-clockwise back toward Red Lodge and Roberts (which is around the time Bob Kero's cow lost the tip of her tail), after which they headed for the mouth of the Stillwater via the West Rosebud, where lo and behold, they found Junior, still waiting.

It's worth noting that, when Smith spots the five wolves on January 9th, they're within easy lope of a large herd of cattle, just as they have been off and on during every other trip through this country. Again, there's no incident, no killing of cows either for fun or profit. I continue to be thick-headed enough to think of that kind of thing as the real story—the horrible event that doesn't happen despite dire predictions to the contrary. Not so. Tonight one of the Billings television stations runs an "exclusive" with the residents of Fishtail, chronicling how terrified everyone is. One woman says the wolves have absolutely destroyed the former peace of the valley, while a sixth grader explains that his father no longer lets him wait for the bus or run around the countryside without his trusty dog or his 22. I keep waiting for the newscasters to mention to their viewers that in all of North America there's never been a single case of a healthy wolf attacking a human. That there are some two thousand wolves running around now in northern Minnesota, at least seven packs in western Montana, about 40,000 animals in Canada, five to seven thousand in Alaska, and barring a rare case of rabies, not a single one of them has ever stolen a kid, chased off a couple out for a walk, taken a bite out of anyone. That happens now and then with mountain lions, of course; on rare occasions with grizzlies. But not with wolves. Not once. Yet on this broadcast, like most, that kind of perspective—that reassurance—never comes.

Meanwhile, would-be poets are turning the Soda Butte wolves into the stuff of legend. In a January issue of the *Agri-News*, Jenny Anders from Fishtail comes up with a run of verse called "The Tale of Wolf Recovery," which is basically a load of buckshot against the feds. I particularly like the last stanza, which transports me back to simpler times as a child, at bedtime, my dear mother reading to me from the Brothers Grimm:

The consequences seem dire, to anyone who's heard,
For now we all realize we can't quite trust the official word.
They finally concede, "We don't know where the wolf will run."   *131*
As the wolf winks, grinning, "Remember, I've just begun."

Even more stirring is an offering titled "His Jaws are Dripping Blood," from Gwen Peterson, purported to be "the official song of the Wolf Alert Patrol," which is to be "sung proudly to the tune of Battle Hymn of the Republic." Eleven verses in all, each punctuated by a rousing chorus of the three usual lines of "Glory, glory, hallelujah," followed by "Their jaws are dripping blood." One of the verses carries Chad McKittrick past even his own fantasies, casting him as a hapless rancher arrested for shooting a wolf. From there she moves on to describe how "We'll feed 'em pets and livestock and a kid or two or three," and finally, this big finish (readers, please feel free to sing along):

> They'll circle round our campfires as they stalk us in the night
> They'll circle round our campfires as they stalk us in the night
> They'll circle round our campfires as they stalk us in the night,
> And wolves will march right on.

You know, I've always kind of liked that song—the original, I mean. This version, though, seems a little startling. Creepy. A kind of literary flag burning.

R   R   R   R   R

Back in Yellowstone the Rose Creek wolves, now ten in number, spend much of their time in the country around the Hellroaring

Overlook, West Boulder Lake, and Specimen Ridge Trailhead, while the Crystal pack is for the most part roaming the east end of the Lamar Valley, often near the confluence of Soda Butte Creek. You may recall Crystal pack's number Six, one of three sub-adults who was bouncing around a meadow last October in a grand reunion with his brother, number Eight, shortly after Eight had taken on the role of mate and step-dad to Nine and her pups. It was Six who seemed either slow or reluctant to take the hint that Nine was upset about that bit of glad-handing between the brothers, the one unwilling to accept that he wasn't welcome around her pups until both Eight and Nine finally chased him off.

As it happens Six is also fond of pushing the envelope in other ways, such as improper tussling with number Five, the alpha female of his own pack. On December 29th, wolf project volunteer Nathan Varley spots Six with the alpha pair in the east end of the Lamar Valley, just south of the confluence of the Lamar River and Soda Butte Creek. After a run of long, slow wails of howling from the alpha female, she gets up and makes a short amble to the north, finally bedding down on the sage flats near a clump of aspen. Six approaches her, seems to nudge her out of her bed, at which point she gets up and strolls away. Two days later Varley spots him tossing a leg over her back in what could be an attempt to mount her, an advance she quickly rebuffs. A minute later he tries again, and this time Five wheels around violently, her teeth bared in a no-nonsense show of aggression. Four, watching these shenanigans from a distance, moves closer to his mate and beds down roughly ten yards away; Six gets the message and moves off by himself, settling a good hundred yards from the alpha pair. As the weeks stretch on toward mid winter, increasingly Six will act like a command animal, as often as not well in the lead of the alpha female, with number Four—the alpha male—trailing, sometimes looking like he's barely got enough gas in the tank for the ride.

In a sense both Four's apparent lack of enthusiasm and Six's abundance of it don't come as any surprise. Four, after all, has never been what you'd call overly aggressive. And besides that, he's thought to be among the oldest wolves ever brought to Yellowstone; in truth last year his age was at times a source of banter between biologists, who said they were just praying he'd have enough oomph to make it to February, for one last coupling with his mate.

Six, though, is one of those wolves with a driven, restless personality, traits he showed way back in Alberta, shortly after being captured. When that operation first got underway wolves were held in individual chain link kennels, inside of which had been placed a metal transport crate, allowing each animal a secluded place to hide. High-spirited number Six, though, must have thought that metal box some kind of chew toy. One day at thirty-five below zero he ripped from the crate a welded frame holding a piece of wire mesh in place across a ventilating hole, hurting himself badly, ripping open three-inch gashes on either side of his mouth. The veterinarian sutured these cuts, but for a time there was real concern among the recovery team as to whether or not he'd open them again, possibly causing an even more serious injury.

One thing Six never lost is his fondness for sparring with bison, running them at every opportunity, just like he did last summer. Recently he managed to cut a small animal from a herd and chase it for about five seconds before finally being driven off by a large adult, who came at him with tail raised, ready to rumble. Another day he stumbled across cow/calf bison pairs in the upper Lamar, moving along slowly, single file, toward a larger group; something spurred the bison into loping, and when they did Six decided the time was right for chase. When these bison reached the larger group the lot of them turned around and lined up shoulder to shoulder, facing Six,

advancing on him, making a wall of bad temper that could make a
football defensive line look like a bunch of milksops. To his credit,
though, even Six knows when to call it quits; as if he'd accomplished
his goal at that point, he turned and moved off fifteen or twenty
yards from the bison, sat down, and wagged his tail.

134

The Crystal pack continues to make regular kills. During a
steady snow on January 2nd, the pack starts running a large herd of
elk in the upper end of the valley, number Six in the lead, followed
by his brother, Two, and finally the alpha pair. On seeing the wolves,
the elk first huddle closer together and then head upslope into the
trees; once in the woods they break loose and scatter in all directions. While Six is busy gauging this bit of bedlam, another group
of elk suddenly appears over a small rise, looking agitated, confused.
In the blink of an eye the young wolf breaks off and gives full chase
to this new bunch of animals, disappearing for a moment into the
woods, then blasting out into the open below treeline to within
fifteen feet of an adult cow. Pouring on the juice he races around to
the front end of the elk, makes two or three great lunges, finally sets
his teeth in the animal's neck; over a period of three, maybe four
seconds he wrestles with the animal, which is still standing, then
finally pulls it down. It doesn't move again. (Despite no end of stories to the contrary, one thing wolves rarely do in bringing down
wild animals is attempt to hamstring them, since doing so would
expose them to a dangerous, even deadly kick from rear hooves.) Six
takes a couple bites from the flesh around the abdomen, but within
a few minutes the alpha female shows up, and so he moves off to let
her feed. After eating their fill the wolves move away from the kill,
heading upslope, peeling off one at a time, the alpha pair followed
by the sub-adults. No sooner do they leave than those quintessential
wolf watchers, the ravens, gather near the carcass by the dozen—
ghostly, charcoal-colored lumps flapping in the falling snow. Just as

magpies have long been observed trailing packs of coyotes as they go about hunting elk calves, ravens tend to be the shadows of wolves, following them over considerable distances for the chance to scavenge their prey. Six, though, seems to have little patience for ravens taking free lunches on his kill, and soon comes bounding down the hill to chase them all away.

This is how wolves typically feed on the carcasses of their kills—eat for a time and then bed down nearby (or if close to a road, out of sight), to return hours later or even the next day to resume feeding. Researchers in other places have even watched wolves burying chunks of meat under the snow, "caching" them for later, though given the number of scavenging species in Yellowstone—from bears to ravens to coyotes—it's hard to imagine there would be anything left of such booty. Indeed, while working with wolves on Isle Royale, Doug Smith always included the percentage of the carcass they had consumed in his field data; given the amount of scavenging by other animals here in Yellowstone, however, such estimations aren't even attempted. With this cycle of eating and resting, in years past people have stumbled onto partially eaten wolf kills and jumped to the conclusion that the wolf is "wasting" much of what he kills, which in turn may have fueled the notion that wolves are out there killing for the fun of it. (That said, although not common, there have certainly been instances, especially at the end of a harsh winter when ungulates are weak, when wolves will occasionally engage in so-called "surplus killing," taking more than they can manage to eat.)

Within minutes of Six bringing down the cow elk, about a mile to the west wolf number Two makes a kill of his own, and is himself busy feeding. A couple hours after this take, Two lets loose with a couple good howls, which encourages the other members of his pack to abandon their own carcass and start moving slowly toward him, heading west along the treeline. And then something

136

remarkable happens—a striking glimpse into the fate that often awaits coyotes bold enough to meddle in what was supposed to be a dinner for wolves. Twenty minutes after the last wolf leaves the first kill and heads west to join Two and the others, a group of coyotes that have been watching from a high hill to the northeast move down to feed on the carcass. At first it's hard to tell just what scatters them from their prize, sends them running off through the storm at a full gallop. But there, just above them, are wolves, running like phantoms through a heavy curtain of falling snow, the Crystal alpha pair as well as Six and Two, racing toward the carcass like a well-oiled posse pulling an ambush on a bunch of rustlers. Six sets his sights on one of the coyotes, chases it north toward the highway with the rest of his pack barely ten yards behind and closing. Clearly running for his life, the coyote reaches the brink of a stream cut some fifteen feet high, leaps off the precipice in true Butch Cassidy-style, lands in the drifted snow, and flounders there. Six quickly works his way down the same embankment, catches the coyote in his front paws, at which point coyote springs up, lowers his head, arches his back, bares his teeth. Not much of a fight really, but you've got to hand it to him, he's giving it his best shot trying to look intimidating. Just as the rest of the pack reaches the edge of the bank a filmmaker, rushing to grab and set up his equipment, lets the tailgate of his car fall with a crash, causing the wolves to pause in the middle of the fight. Coyote senses his chance, bolts down the frozen creek, and this time Six doesn't chase. Coyote owes that filmmaker big time.

Whatever lessons coyotes may stand to gain from such encounters about the dangers of feeding on wolf kills, hunger will always be there to drive them right back again, push them to take any chance for a full belly. Three hours later, there are four coyotes back on the same carcass; whether they include that lucky fellow who barely escaped with his life earlier in the afternoon, it's hard to say. Once again the coyotes scatter with the coming of the four wolves, three running east through the open flats, and one heading west, into the timber. It's that one coyote running into the woods that the wolves decide to pursue, and again, it's number Six that brings him down. But while Six seems content to play with the coyote, swat it about with its massive paws, when the alpha male arrives he has only business on his mind. He attacks the coyote with forceful bites on the back, neck, and rear; soon the alpha female appears as well, and she too attacks with gusto, an act that seems to give Six the motivation he needs to join in and do the same. The coyote fights back for all he's worth, rising to bite at his aggressors long after one would have thought him surely dead, but it's no use. The three wolves give the coyote a final round of bites, a last bit of shaking, drop him on the snow, and walk away. The next day, January 3rd, coyotes will be back on the carcass again, and still another one will die.

In all, from November through February of 1996—that time of pair bonding, scent marking, and mating in both wolves and coyotes—researchers will document twelve coyote deaths at the jaws of wolves, all but one of which are at or near wolf-killed elk. Direct observations by Bob Crabtree and his researchers tell us these deaths were the result of wolves either returning to defend their kill, or returning for a second or a third feeding only to find coyotes scavenging the carcasses. (While it might seem that one or two wolves would have no trouble dispatching even a whole handful of coyotes, the wolves seem wary enough to always play the numbers; every kill witnessed so far has involved three or more wolves on a single coyote.) Extrapolating from the number of dead coyotes actually found near wolf-killed ungulates, Crabtree estimates that in a two-month period from December through February, 1996, from the fifteen coyote packs present in these wolf-popuated areas, three dozen coyotes have died. "Half the coyote packs in the Lamar Valley are disrupted," he says. "Vocalization is way down. There's no alpha pair scent marking, which would suggest a decline in breeding activity. Three of the ten packs have disintegrated." Though it's impossible to say for certain, at this point it looks as though the decline of coyote packs in the Lamar Valley could reach as high as twenty-five percent.

Coyotes and elk aren't the only ones being chased by wolves. On January 10th, Crystal members Two and Six burst out in the open, heading southeast across the valley, not far from Theater Creek—this time bolting after a cow moose. While the two wolves manage to close to within less than twenty yards of their prey, that's as close as they ever manage to get. In what proves to be a wonderful flash of cleverness, the moose plunges into the middle of a group of about a hundred elk gathered near Chalcedony Creek, causing mass turmoil in the herd, scattering animals in every direction; the moose then quietly disappears in the midst of the confusion.

Due in part to the openness of the country here and the sheer abundance of prey, a lot of the hunting by wolves in the Lamar Valley has a certain random, churning quality to it—wolves loping along through open meadows, spotting a herd of elk, then kicking into a chase. But wolves are also extremely good at catching direct scent of prey several hundred yards or more upwind. At that point all the animals in the pack will stop, and eyes, ears, and noses will turn toward the prey; from there the pack may begin moving in the direction of the scent, relying on restrained, stalking-style movements to get as close as they can before launching their attack. Wolves are also good at picking up the scent not of the animal itself, but of the fresh tracks it leaves behind. It's easy to imagine the Soda Butte pack, for instance, traveling through the lodgepole forests north of Cooke City and crossing the track of a moose or deer that passed through not long before. If they happen to be in the mood to hunt—

and that's not always the case—likely they'd then follow the track line with noses to the ground, working intently but cautiously to close the gap, if necessary even maneuvering to stay downwind from the prey, until reaching a place from which to attempt the kill. That attempt, in turn, usually consists of actions that are more or less trademarks of wolf hunting—a fast rush, and a short chase.

139

Just how often the Yellowstone wolves kill seems to be related to the number of animals in the group. Based on numbers compiled in the spring and fall of 1995, on average the Crystal pack, with five wolves, was killing every five to six days; Soda Butte, when it had six members, took prey animals about every 3.5 days; and since Rose Creek swelled to nine members, it was making kills about every other day. Those rates increased somewhat over the winter. Most biologists assume the wolf population in greater Yellowstone will settle at about 100 animals. Based on the kill rates recorded up to March of 1996, each year 100 wolves would take roughly eight percent, or about 1,600 of the 20,000 elk that make up the northern herds. (Some ungulate herds, of course, depending on where they live, will be more significantly affected than others.) That's not far off the mark from what was originally predicted in the Environmental Impact Statement.

And yet it's hardly as tidy as all that. Thanks in large part to the sheer unpredictability of wolves, the number of ungulates that will end up being taken in this ecosystem continues to be a topic of heated debate. Some scientists, men like prominent Alaskan wolf biologist Bill Gasaway, believe that the Fish and Wildlife Service and the National Park Service woefully underestimated the number of elk that wolf packs in the Yellowstone ecosystem will take in the years to come. Gasaway has focused his studies on wolf/moose interactions in Alaska, and has made a pretty convincing case that moose populations there are being kept at roughly one-fifth to one-tenth of what they'd be if wolves weren't in the equation.

140

Basically ungulate populations are regulated by two factors: the available food supply, and predation. If the moose Gasaway is studying, for example, were pushing the upper limits of the available food supply, they'd be said to have reached "carrying capacity." The consequences of living above carrying capacity include lowered reproduction and survival rates, as well as increased incidence of disease—all of which, over time, tend to bring the population back down again. There can also be serious impacts on the environment when a population lives above carrying capacity, including various plant communities being badly over browsed or grazed. On the other hand, if animals live below carrying capacity they tend to enjoy high reproduction rates, high survival for adults, and general health and vigor throughout the population. While the moose in Gasaway's study clearly are not at carrying capacity, when it comes to Yellowstone's elk, it's hard to be certain one way or the other. In fact one of the greatest debates of modern times seems to be whether or not the elk populations in and around the park are above carrying capacity. One school of thought, known as the "theory of natural regulation," says the environment will limit elk numbers before they cause too much damage to the land. Others maintain that, before long, elk will overrun the ecosystem altogether.

And there are other, more regional factors that make Gasaway's somewhat dire predictions uncertain. Biologists like Doug Smith are quick to point out that Yellowstone is not Alaska, and elk are not moose. (Given that, up until now, elk have been living on a fairly small portion of the North American wolf range, how these two animals are going to interact with one another is still very much a matter of guesswork.) What's more, plant productivity, Smith says, is significantly higher at the more southerly latitudes of Yellowstone, where the growing season lasts much longer than it does in Alaska.

Further, moose are primarily browsers, which means they feed mostly on the foliage of woody plants; elk, by comparison, are predominantly grazers. Roughly eighty percent of the Northern Range offers grazing, while only about ten percent is browsing habitat.

That brings us to the next regulator, predation, which in turn brings us to wolves. Interestingly enough, when wolves are the only predators in the puzzle, moose seem to do just fine. In fact at Isle Royal, where wolves are the only predator to worry about, moose populations have at various times actually gotten larger, not smaller. But many biologists, such as Gasaway, feel that when you have multiple predators, the game changes dramatically. In Yellowstone, for example, elk will be contending not just with predation on calves by wolves, but also bears (not to mention coyotes, golden eagles, etc.); in places like Slough Creek, popular with both wolves and grizzlies, the calving season could end up being an incredibly challenging time for elk. Then for adult elk there are mountain lions to throw into the mix, as well as a long line of hunters just the other side of the park boundary. Of course you can't launch the argument of how much Yellowstone's elk might suffer from multiple predators, without acknowledging that wolves here have the option of multiple prey. In short, a tangle of variables. All in all, most biologists predict that the addition of wolves to the ecosystem will reduce elk numbers at least five percent, and possibly as much as twenty or even thirty percent in some areas. Gasaway takes a much more extreme position, saying we may be looking at a fifty-percent decline in elk populations over twenty-five years. *If* there is a fifty-percent taking, and *if* it results in a steady decline of Northern Range elk populations, then one way of dealing with it might be to change hunting practices outside the park, greatly reducing the take of females. In the worst-case scenario, even a ten-percent take of cows by hunters might be too much, which of course wouldn't exactly be greeted as good news by sportsmen.

One more critical thing to keep in mind about Gasaway's number crunching has to do once again with that long-standing debate about carrying capacity: are Yellowstone's elk living at carrying capacity, or below it? That's incredibly important, because if elk are above carrying capacity—and many think they are—removing ten animals would have the effect of actually freeing up food resources so that, roughly speaking, ten elk would survive someplace else. This is what biologists refer to as "compensatory mortality." It's only if the herds are below carrying capacity that taking those ten elk would actually translate into ten animals being removed from the total number of elk in the population.

The mystery of wolves continues to divide biologists and their theories. Men like Francois Messier of Canada and Rolf Peterson, a noted wolf researcher on Isle Royale for twenty-six years, are also saying that both the future total number of wolves and their effect on elk may have been underestimated, though they make their cases for different reasons than Gasaway. Peterson says the final picture will be painted to no small degree by how vulnerable elk happen to be at any given time. An elk population filled with young, healthy adults, for example, will likely be able to stave off attacks by wolves fairly well. But there are other factors to consider when talking about vulnerability. A couple harsh winters, for example, when severe weather and deep snow weaken ungulates, might lead to wolves pushing elk into periods of significant decline.

The bottom line at this point is that nobody really knows, nor will they for a long time to come. It could take ten years for the average number of wolves to be reached in the Yellowstone ecosystem, and yet another ten or more to reach any kind of equilibrium with the prey base. What I find especially troubling is that, thanks to a thorough trashing by Congress of funding for scientific research,

here we stand in Yellowstone at a historic moment in wildlife resto-
ration, and so little is being done to build a foundation of knowledge
for sound management in the future. "If there's another Isle Royale, *143*
this should be it," says Doug Smith, referring to thirty-eight years of
stellar, unbroken predator-prey research on that island in Lake
Superior. So far at Yellowstone, though, with few exceptions the
classroom is open but the seats are empty. Of course a number of
biologists are more than a little upset about this, frantic that this
golden opportunity is slipping through their fingers; some are launching unprecedented efforts to raise research moneys through private
sources. On one hand I commend them for seeing the writing on
the wall; privately-funded science, after all, is better than no science
at all. Yet I can't help but wonder whether the day may come when
large donors are going to be the only ones sitting behind the wheel
driving the scientific agenda. Somehow, as a kid in school, I never
thought that standing on the threshold of the twenty-first century
the idea of knowledge for knowledge's sake would be lying flat
on the ground, gasping for breath, some quaint notion from days
gone by.

ELEVEN

Five days before Christmas, it's natural selection with a strange, modern twist in the upper Lamar Valley, when one of the Rose Creek pups runs full speed into the side of a UPS truck and kills himself. The impact of the crash is so severe the pup's face is actually crushed. When examined in Mammoth later that same night, the pup weighs in at seventy pounds. His coat has changed from that dark, somewhat homogenous coloring of youth into a striking, beautiful collage of black and silver and rust. A couple nights after the event, I'm surfing the Internet and happen across a couple self-styled wolf lovers talking about how the UPS driver was a wolf hater who went out of his way to run down that poor pup. In fact not only did the pup run into that truck all by himself, actually hitting the rear corner of the vehicle, but the driver was depressed damned near to tears.

Elsewhere, number Seven continues to roam. Perfectly content to be a solo act, as she's been from the time she and her mother, number Nine, and her step-father, the great, star-crossed number Ten, all wandered out of the Rose Creek pen some eight months ago. Even from the air you can tell she's hearty, big and fit and full, an alpha female in the making if ever there was one. "I just won't believe it if she doesn't end up mated this winter," says Rolf Peterson during his autumn sabbatical in Yellowstone. "She's just too perfect. Too perfect." Around New Year's Day biologists spotted Seven at Buffalo Creek, which is just west of that stretch of the Lamar Valley where the Crystal pack has been thoroughly entrenched for the past month, nabbing elk from the five hundred or so milling around there these days. As of late there have been only four Crystal wolves visible from the Lamar Road, instead of the usual five. Where the missing member is—a two-year-old male known as number Three— nobody has a clue, especially since he happens to be the one wolf whose radio transmitter goes on the fritz now and then, the thing crackling and making thumping sounds during one flyover two weeks ago, altogether silent the next. Doug Smith and Mike Phillips are swooning like matchmakers, hoping hard that he'll head far enough west to make the acquaintance of the fabulous Ms. Seven.

On an altogether different level of roaming are the adventures of that traveling fool, the black, splay-footed Soda Butte male, num-ber Twelve. You may recall that after meeting with ranchers north of Red Lodge on January 8th, Doug Smith flew and found the Soda Butte pack near Fishtail, back with the pup but minus number Twelve. Incredibly, the following week reports come in of a black, wolf-like animal forty miles southwest of Cody, in the South Fork country, a wild slice of largely national forest land on the east side of the Absaroka Mountains; that this is the missing number Twelve is confirmed a few days later on a flight by Mike Phillips. It's a long, rugged roam of some seventy to ninety miles to get from Fishtail to the upper South Fork, no matter what your choice of routes. The more crooked path carries you around the Beartooth Front and then across a long sweep of high sagebrush desert, finally crossing the Clark Fork and Shoshone rivers. The more direct route, on the other hand, which is by no means out of the question for this traveler, runs up and over the ten-thousand-foot-high plateaus that form the roof of the Beartooth Mountains, down into the Sunlight Basin, then either out to the high desert or up and over more rough and tattered high country, through deep woods to the Shoshone River, and finally up the South Fork. From the air, or even standing on some choice overlook like Dead Indian Pass, the ruggedness of this country seems overwhelming.

The whole business of dispersal—how and why animals move out from their place of birth—is one of the more fundamental pillars of wolf science. Wrapped up in the theories is this question of how, in such a tightly bonded, socially oriented species, certain individual wolves end up leaving the group to seek their fortunes elsewhere. Of course sometimes the leaving can be a matter of a limited food supply, a case where a subordinate animal ends up being pushed to the end of a somewhat Spartan buffet line, and out of desperation goes to seek food elsewhere. Exactly how fast a weaker animal reaches the end of that short stick can depend to some extent on what the prey happens to be. A typical pack size for wolves feeding primarily on deer and elk, for instance, is five to seven animals; if you happen to be wolf number eight in a place with limited prey, and not exactly the most robust member of the group, things may go sour for you fast. For wolves feeding on larger animals, though, say moose, the pack size may be larger, eight or ten or in a few cases even fifteen. (The higher numbers seem to be less a matter of needing more animals to take down the prey—the very youngest members of the pack, after all, are pretty worthless when it comes to such a skilled task—than that there's simply more food available for every kill made, which supports more animals.) At any rate, given the abundance of prey in this ecosystem, the size of the Soda Butte pack, and the lack of competing predators, food supply would hardly have been a problem for Twelve.

Some say young wolves leave because they get pushed out by their parents. But that may be true only on occasion, such as during the breeding season when aggression is running high, when an alpha wolf might become agitated over the possibility of a younger animal being a competitor for breeding rights. Whether that's relevant to Twelve is hard to say. True, a few female wolves have been known to come into proestrus as early as the first week in January, but the peak of breeding season is much later, around the third week in February—long after Twelve struck out on his own. What's more, if parents were the primary driving factor in wolf dispersal you'd expect to find young wolves leaving within a fairly narrow age range, say eight to sixteen months. But in fact the window for dispersing wolves is broad, stretching from as young as ten months to several years. This indicates a certain tolerance of young by adults. In a sense, the wolf family can be thought of as a springboard from which many animals have the luxury of making the decision to leave or to stay, and if they do go, whether to stay away or come back home again (at least if he or she isn't in competition for the alpha slot). Still another factor in this decision is whether there's a place to disperse *to;* if the land all around has holes in it—opportunities to find mates and establish territory—a wolf prone to dispersal is more likely to go. If, on the other hand, the world around her is filled up with intact packs, she may not.

"It's a little strange," Doug Smith says about the timing of Twelve's departure. "January is typically when wolves stick together— a time when the cohesiveness of the pack tends to be high. The pups are traveling. If a wolf is going to move on, it usually happens in late winter, February through April." It's interesting to speculate whether that more normal late-winter dispersal may have something to do with the fact that, in typical situations with established packs and little unoccupied habitat, a wolf traveling in early winter would encounter intact, cohesive groups—animals fully capable of defending their territories. By leaving later, females are getting toward denning. The most sedentary time of year is approaching, when wolves operate more in pairs, even as singles. Exactly the kind of structure that would pose less of a threat to a strange wolf traveling through unknown territory.

149

As it turns out Twelve's little jaunt to the South Fork is just the beginning. On January 16th, Doug Smith flies again, and this time finds Twelve well to the southeast, not far from the town of Dubois, Wyoming. At this point he seems beyond mere wandering into something closer to nomadism. It isn't that wolves traveling such distances is unheard of. But up until now wolf studies have almost always focused in places where a lone animal wouldn't leave the pack without running into other wolves. Far-ranging movements are often spurred by the fact that surrounding territories are so saturated with full packs that the loner is forced to keep moving, putting on lots of miles before finding a place to settle. (Studies suggest that in those more normal circumstances, with other wolves in the area, a sub-adult like Twelve would have roughly a two-in-three chance of settling and pairing with a female.) But to go on and on through the country, expecting to see other wolves and not finding hide nor hair of them, well that's something very strange indeed. It remains to be seen whether Twelve will at some point call it quits, turn around, and head back to the Yellowstone country, or whether he'll just keep going, wandering, never mating and never coming home, living out his days as a so-called "lone wolf."

No matter why he left, the fact that Twelve is venturing so far and wide in search of a mate brings into serious question the long-standing claim by some that there was a significant number of wolves already in this ecosystem. The fact is that after nine months of freedom, not a single one of the new wolves in and around Yellowstone has ever been seen in the company of an uncollared animal.

It'll be interesting to see how Twelve's two sub-adult pack mates react to his leaving. They too, after all, may be feeling the urge to go. Will they look around now, though, decide that one less pack mate leaves them in an awfully good position—firmly rooted in a small pack, surrounded by deer, elk, and moose—and in the end decide to stay?

Twelve's leaving does at least solve one puzzle. Obviously he wasn't the alpha male of the Soda Butte group, as biologists once thought, or he wouldn't be out there running around on his own. That distinction must instead go to wise old "Blue"—the Gray Ghost.

＊　＊　＊　＊　＊

As it turns out, Twelve isn't the only sub-adult that's decided to engage in a bit of rounding. The last time researchers located number Three, a sub-adult from the Crystal Pack, was in late December, at the east end of the Lamar Valley, running the home drainage with his pack mates, back and forth across the patchwork of meadow and woodlands between Flint and Calfee, Soda and Pebble creeks. And then he was gone. This is the missing wolf that the recovery team has been hoping would eventually show up with that lone female, number Seven. No such luck. During the week of January 8th, Animal Damage Control officer Jim Hoover gets a call from ranchers in the Paradise Valley, near Emigrant. One of their sheep is dead, Susan Brailsford explains. What's more, there's a large black wolf in the area skulking around, scaring her guard dogs, sending them running with their tails between their legs to cower on the porch. Hoover answers the call, tunes in his tracking receiver, finds number Three right where the woman claimed he was, just a short lope from the ranch. The Park recovery team has its fingers crossed, hoping the situation will resolve itself, that Three will turn tail and head back south to Yellowstone. Then on Friday another sheep is dead. The next day Three is back in the Gardiner area, but on Sunday he does a U-turn, heads north again, back to the ranch.

Doug Smith is on the ground above and behind the ranch when the plane comes overhead late that afternoon—a spotting plane, fixing the location of the wolf so that helicopter pilot Rick Sandford can maneuver his craft in close enough for Hoover to fire net guns over the wolf. "He flushed out of the ravine and came up the hill right toward us," Smith says. "Stopped right across the gully. There's no doubt about it, this guy was in a very bad spot." Three is busted, taken to Gardiner, and examined; he weighs in at ninety-five pounds and seems to be in good health. After a physical check-up he's flown off to the Rose Creek jail, back to eating those disgusting prison rations of half-frozen carcasses that the humans keep dragging in. The choice Mike Phillips faces is whether to let him go, or grant his desire for a mate by providing a mail-order bride from the new batch of wolves arriving soon from British Columbia. Get him hitched, have some pups, cool his urge to roam.

The more I look at the circumstances behind Three's arrest, the more convinced I am that, while he's almost surely guilty, here's a case any defense attorney would love. First there's the canine wounds found around the neck of the dead sheep—impossible to say whether they were caused by wolf or dog. Add that to the rather troubling fact that, according to several locals, two Great Pyrenees dogs have been roaming the Paradise Valley killing sheep for some time now. And then that business about the sheep carcass itself; after the initial investigation Park Service officials ask for the remains, but Jim Hoover tells them it won't do them much good. Nothing left, really. Eaten by the guard dog in charge of protecting it.

I can see it now. A federal courtroom in Billings, wolf number Three at the defense table, head hung, looking, er, sheepish. Beginning of the trial, his attorney, a big man with a cheeky face in an ivory-colored suit, handkerchief in his hand, wiping his brow. "Ladies and gentlemen of the jury," he wheezes in a soft southern accent. "I respectfully submit that things are not quite what they appear. That my client, far from being a cold-blooded killer, is but a hapless victim. A victim of our long-standing prejudice against wolves. Picture this with me now if you will. One fine morning this young wolf, this wolf sitting right here in front of you, is out and about, making his way down the Paradise Valley, minding his own business, looking for a mate, trying his level best to become a family man, what with breeding season coming on and all. Now along the way he passes no end of cattle wintering in this valley. But this is no cow killer, ladies and gentlemen. He ignores them. Refuses to have anything to do with them. Then, lo and behold, what should happen not far from the site of this tragic sheep killing but that my client catches scent of that very thing he's been looking for. Other wolves! That's right, I said other wolves. As it turns out these are the famed buffalo wolves belonging to Jack Lynch and Mary Wheeler, sitting in pens less than three miles from the herd of sheep in question. Naturally, my client is excited about what his nose tells him. But confused, too. He's able to howl back and forth with these strangers, but because they're in a pen, he can't really engage them. Kind of like courting beneath the window of what you think is a sorority house, only to discover it's a women's jail. I invite you to look at these photos, taken by Jack Lynch himself on December 26th—the day the Park Service noticed my client was missing—showing number Three just seventy-five yards outside those wolf pens, looking on.

"So he lingers there, mills about, eventually comes on the car-

cass of a dead sheep killed by that villainous pair of dogs, the Great
Pyrenees brothers. Over the course of this trial we'll bring in a number of witnesses, respected citizens, including a long-time resident
outfitter who'll testify that those dogs have been killing sheep in this
part of the valley on a regular basis for months. So my client, this
unfortunate wolf, stumbles across one of these victims, is hungry,
decides to help himself to a lamb chop—after all, if he doesn't take
it those greedy coyotes will—at which point the good Mrs. Brailsford
happens to look out her door and spots him. A simple case of being
in the wrong place at the wrong time."

*   *   *   *   *

Steve Fritts and Ed Bangs with U.S. Fish and Wildlife don't like
the idea of trying to mate Three with a female from Canada;
not a good plan, they say, to use a sheep-killer as the nucleus for a
new pack. What happens if he gets out of the pen, remembers all
about the goodies on that sheep ranch, and goes right back, this
time dragging a bunch of other wolves along with him? Better to
relocate. So roughly a week and a half after arriving back at Rose
Creek, number Three is plucked from the pen and taken to Fishing
Bridge, near Pelican Valley—that high, fingered patchwork of sweeping meadows the Crystal pack was so fond of last summer. When
the kennel box is opened Three doesn't wait around to see if leaving
is the right thing to do. He runs out of that box like a track grey-
hound at the ring of the bell and the flash of the rabbit, though in
truth deep snow forces him to bound away, more like the rabbit
than the dog. Unfortunately, he doesn't really catch on to the purpose of this little relocation, that he's been given a second chance.
Seems to miss the point entirely. During an overflight the following
week, on a Wednesday, biologists locate him at White Lake on the

Mirror Plateau, just north of Pelican Valley; not a bad place, really—still well inside the park. But then he starts to move. On
154 Thursday he's drifted northwest some seventeen miles, to around
Tower Junction. On Friday he's on the move again, still further north,
to Daley Lake. By Saturday he's spotted back near the Brailsford
Ranch, some fifty miles from his release site, and a sheep is crippled
with a bloody bite to the neck. Under the terms of this reintroduction wolves get two strikes, and then they're out.

At 9:49 on a warm Monday morning a helicopter lifts off with
Animal Damage Control officers Jim Hoover and Jim Rost, sails
toward the gully behind the Brailsford's home where number Three
is lying low. Mike Phillips and Doug Smith are on a hilltop above
that ravine, Doug with earphones on and a tracking antenna to better follow the wolf's movements. As the helicopter nears the gully,
Three flushes, and Smith loses the signal as the wolf rounds a bluff,
then regains both sight and sound of him as he pops up on a bench,
still running. At that point the copter zips fast and low toward the
wolf, stops and hovers about fifty yards above him, and Jim Hoover
leans out and fires two shots to turn him. The next two rounds are
for keeps, hitting him full in the body, three pieces of the bird-shot-
style ammunition traveling with so much force they go right through
his quarter-inch-thick, leather-like radio collar. By 9:55, six minutes after the operation began, Three is dead.

In fifteen years of wolf research this is the first time Doug Smith
has ever seen a helicopter shooting. And while he's quick to recognize the necessity of what's just happened, both legally and politically,
still it leaves a bad taste. "I know he wasn't supposed to have a chance,
and he didn't. It'd be like you and me standing out here in this road
with two pitchforks and then having the United States Air Force do
an overflight on us. It's not exactly a fair fight. And that's how it
felt." After the shooting a neighboring rancher drives up slowly, gets

out of his pickup, walks over toward Doug and Mike. He looks to be about eighty—stubbled face, brown and worn as an old man's favorite saddle. He wears buckle-over boots and an unbuttoned jacket.

"Kind of a shame, isn't it?" he says.

Doug looks over at him. "Yeah, it really is."

The old rancher goes on. "I don't think that wolf was hurtin' anybody being here." He turns his head and points up the hill. "When my dad settled this place in 1903, there was a black wolf runnin' up there in those trees. Now a black wolf is back. And you guys are shootin' it." The helicopter has picked up the wolf and sweeps back over to land next to Doug and Mike's pickup to give them the carcass. On spotting the rancher the pilot points down the hill, letting Smith and Phillips know he'll land there instead.

The rancher talks on a bit about the Brailsfords, his neighbors down the gully who came here in 1987, the people who complained about the wolf, demanded something be done. Doesn't care much for them, he says.

"Look," Doug asks the old man. "You want to come down with us and see this wolf?"

"I already saw him. He was by my place, stakin' out territory. Scent markin' up there."

"If that wolf had shown up on that old-timer's place, we never would have known it," Doug says later. "He wouldn't have called anybody."

Predictably, elsewhere around the state, the sheep kills are being used to paint wolf biologists as liars who claimed such things would never happen. In truth I can't find a single public document relative to this project that doesn't say exactly the opposite—that wolves will roam outside the park, that stock depredation will occur. Dave Mech said seventeen years ago that every successful wolf recovery program eventually requires wolf management—in other words, relocating or getting rid of problem animals. (Of course it's a good idea to keep potential losses in perspective. The most comprehensive studies on livestock depredations to date were conducted in Minnesota from 1975 through 1989, a time when there were about 1,500 wolves running around in the northern part of that state. Verified livestock losses during the period averaged thirty-two a year, affecting about one out of every 300 farms. The highest annual cattle losses were 4.5 animals per 10,000, and 26.6 animals per 10,000 sheep. And yes, cattle do occupy open pastures in that part of the country from April to October. Here in the Paradise Valley right now there's actually a small sigh of relief coming from many stockmen, since number Three passed yet again through three separate herds of cattle without giving them a second look. He also passed by a dead horse without touching it.)

Biologist Steve Fritts, one of the key players in wolf reintroduction in greater Yellowstone, consistently pointed out that depredation would occur in the Yellowstone area, that it has in fact occurred "wherever wolves and domestic animals have coexisted in North America," and in 1993 wrote a fifty-four page article in a scientific monograph outlining potential problems of livestock depredation from wolves and ways of dealing with them. It was exactly that kind of straight talk from biologists that led to these wolves being declared a non-essential, experimental population under the Endangered Species Act, which makes it easier to relocate or destroy problem animals.

As chance would have it, wolf Three takes the bullet on the same day it's announced that Pat Williams, respected veteran congressman of twenty years and as big a political personality as you'll find in the state of Montana, is retiring. You would of course expect such an event to be front page news in the *Billings Gazette,* and it is.

But the greatest number of column inches goes not to Williams, but right back where it's been for the past several days. To the story of a problem wolf.

*   *   *   *   *

There are, thankfully, a couple of bright spots on the horizon. The Soda Butte pack has left the West Rosebud country in the early days of calving season to return to their old stomping grounds up the Stillwater, around Wounded Man Creek. (That champion wanderer from their ranks, number Twelve—the wolf last seen near Dubois, Wyoming—hasn't been spotted or heard from for weeks now, even though Grand Teton National Park workers have been putting on their tracking ears whenever they head out on overflights. "I guess no news is good news," Doug Smith says half-heartedly.)

But the best news is happening well to the southwest of the Stillwater. In the third week of January, that dandy little wolf number Seven joined up with one of the young bachelors from the Crystal pack, exactly as all those matchmakers on the wolf recovery team thought and hoped she would. The lucky male—and I do mean lucky, because Seven is without question the catch of the park—is number Two, the wolf who hung back from the rest of the Crystal pack after leaving the pen, roaming on his own for most of April, rejoining the group again full time in late August. So far these two seem content to hang out around Seven's old stomping grounds at Blacktail Plateau—a place rich with wildlife, and even more significant given recent events, well inside the park. If this couple breeds they'll create the first naturally occurring pack in Yellowstone National Park; the recovery team has decided they'll be known as the Leopold Pack, in honor of Aldo Leopold, one of the world's great conservation biologists.

The possibility of these two homesteading brings to mind questions about the day when Yellowstone wolves will have adjacent territories. Does it make a difference in how well they get along if one of the animals used to be a member of the adjacent pack? Are wolves like the extended human families that have existed in the remote holes and hollers of the east, where social customs made it possible for the right marriage to soften the urge to feud? A remarkable example of just that can be found on Isle Royale, where virtually every wolf pack has at least one relative somehow related to the next. There it's not unusual for the related animal to return to her natal territory now and then. When she does, though, she may leave the unrelated mate standing outside along the fringe of her old family's turf. It's even been recorded where the related wolf will go into the natal territory, grab a meal with the old gang of relatives, then walk back out to rejoin her mate, at which point the two of them will cruise off again together. What an incredibly civilized way to visit relatives.

Most researchers seem to think the northeastern tier of the park near the Lamar Valley will eventually support four to six packs of wolves. If Two and Seven decide to settle and raise young on the Blacktail Plateau, their pups may well hook up with offspring of Rose Creek (now located about twelve miles to the east), or the offspring of Crystal, located in the Lamar Valley, which would eventually lead to exclusive territories being created in the open spaces that now exist between the packs. It's also possible that territories will change in this part of Yellowstone during the cold months to allow everyone better access to the high numbers of wintering elk. This is precisely what happens every year at Wood Buffalo National Park in Alberta, where wolves feed almost exclusively on bison. There during winter much of the normal territory structure breaks down, allowing five or six packs to converge on a concentration of several thousand bison. Not working together, exactly, but certainly using a less structured system for the benefit of all.

One final slice of good news has to do with the fact that this winter we're seeing one of the biggest migrations of the northern elk herd out of the park in recorded history. One of the big concerns biologists have had all along is whether or not the Yellowstone wolves would follow these elk migrations, and in the process end up smack dab in the middle of ranching country. And while one day that could still be an issue, the fact is that right now not a single wolf has elected to follow these winter migrations. Everyone is staying put; thoroughly content, it would seem, to prey on the large numbers of elk that yet remain.

*　　*　　*　　*　　*

February. The beginning of the very first breeding season in the wilds of Yellowstone. Seven and her new partner, number Two, still roaming the Blacktail Plateau, seem perfect candidates for parenthood. As do the Soda Butte pair, which bred and produced one surviving pup last spring, and number Nine, who with Ten gave birth to those eight beautiful pups—seven blacks and one gray— outside of Red Lodge. Everyone has their fingers crossed that Crystal will breed, too. Crunching the numbers for just the free-ranging wolves, the ecosystem stands to grow at best by four litters of pups, which at full litter size would mean roughly two dozen animals. If you toss in even one other litter from the four groups of seventeen new wolves still in the acclimation pens, it's conceivable that by late this spring there could be some sixty-five animals running around greater Yellowstone.

Wolves enjoy a relatively long period of courtship, which includes "snuffling" (a nipping around the lips, much as when pups

160

try to encourage adults to regurgitate food for them), and a gentle grabbing of snouts. There's also some evidence that, as mating time approaches, there's less and less distance between the alphas when they curl up to rest. Furthermore, female wolves tend to be in heat for a long time, with the actual period when they're receptive to the male lasting some two weeks. Taken together these kinds of behaviors almost certainly have the effect of creating powerful psychological bonds between breeding animals. And for wolves that's especially important. Because the real benefit of behaviors that encourage the alpha pair to stay together—sometimes even for life—is the added measure of solidarity that spills over from that relationship into the rest of the pack.

TWELVE

Number Twelve, Splayfoot, that greatest of the Yellowstone wanderers, is dead. Found on February 12th on a road-side near Daniel, Wyoming, sixty miles east of the Idaho line and some hundred and sixty miles south of the Stillwater country where he last spent time with his companions of the Soda Butte group. He's the fourth wolf to die, the fourth death related to humans. Not counting that eight-month-old pup who managed to run headlong into the side of a UPS truck out in the Lamar Valley, each of the mortalities has occurred outside Yellowstone National Park—one to the northeast, near Red Lodge, one north in the Paradise Valley near Emigrant, and now Twelve, in the far southern reaches of the ecosystem. The Environmental Impact Statement actually predicted a ten-percent loss of animals over the first year due to various causes; and again, the recovery team never expected pups to be born until the spring of 1996. So whereas we should have had about a dozen free-ranging animals ten months into this reintroduction, we in fact have nineteen. Yet I'm finding it hard to be overly enthusiastic about that success. Maybe it's because the deaths of Three and Twelve came so close together. That, combined with the fact that

Twelve's sister, number Eleven, has disappeared without a trace. Finally, there's a growing consensus that the last of the wolves ever to come to Yellowstone by human hand are the ones now sitting in the acclimation pens. I may well be making mountains out of mole-hills, but in these first three weeks of February the whole reintroduction effort seems fragile all over again.

The four groups of seventeen new Canadian wolves waiting in the pens, eleven females and six males, are finally settling down. And not a minute too soon. Several have suffered severe damage to their teeth from chewing on the fence. The toll has been especially high in the alpha male and female at the Nez Perce site as well as both wolves at Blacktail, all of which have lost their lower canines. Most of the damage seems to be the result of constant gnawing on the chain link; incredibly, though, security rangers in the area have also witnessed the Nez Perce wolves making dramatic leaps high off the ground, clamping their teeth eight feet up on the fence and just dangling there for twenty to thirty seconds, die-hards trying to yank down the jailhouse walls. Chewing was to a lesser degree a common problem in the first group of penned wolves too, and last fall recovery team members spent weeks trying to figure out some kind of solution, but never did. It would be next to impossible to devise a system with 650 or more feet of solid panels to rim the circumference of each pen—something that would be both affordable and light enough to be transported to remote sites. Still, nobody expected the problem to be as bad as this. "We brought in young wolves," says Mike Phillips, referring to the wearing of teeth being a sign of age. "We're releasing old ones."

Wolves, of course, live by their teeth. Forty of them: Sixteen premolars and eight molars, which include four self-sharpening "flesh teeth" on each side, used for ripping or cutting tough hide and tendons. Then there are twelve incisors, used for scraping and clipping.

And finally, four canines—what we sometimes refer to as "fangs"—
which are mostly what's being lost or damaged by the fences of the
acclimation pens. The canines are large teeth, over two inches long   *163*
if you include the part embedded in the jaw, and they're what wolves
rely on to grab and hold their prey. There seems little doubt that any
wolf who loses his or her canines will be seriously compromised
when it comes to bringing down large mammals like elk or moose.
Such a loss could be especially problematic for lead animals like the
alpha male and female in the Nez Perce site, since the act of a kill is
often launched by one or both of the alpha pair. Could there be
social consequences if as lead wolves they can no longer play a lead
in killing? Though he was never able to offer any proof, fifty years
ago Stanley Young suggested that one reason an animal may turn
into a "lone wolf" is because excessive tooth wear keeps her from
participating with other pack members in securing food.

Beyond securing food, a wolf's teeth—perhaps especially the
canines—may be an important part of how a dominant animal com-
municates with other members of his or her pack. To see an alpha
male or female with erect ears pointing forward, a wrinkled forehead, an open mouth with the corners pulled forward and bared
teeth, is to see a wolf in full threat posture; that imposing look,
combined with other signs, such as a tail raised above the flat of the
back, is a key to how alpha wolves preserve the social rankings within
the pack. There's a common misunderstanding that wolves maintain order through all kinds of intra-pack squabbling and fighting
for position. Nothing could be farther from the truth. Over millions of years wolves have evolved a complex set of posturing rituals
that can be used to get a wide range of messages across—showing
restraint, submissiveness, authority, depression, or self confidence—
without unnecessary risk of injury. Posturing in wolves, just like
so-called "body language" in humans, is the behavioral framework

that allows their complex social system to function. A wolf snarling without canines might result in other animals not taking it seriously, kind of like a guy with his arm in a cast picking bar fights.

No one really knows why these new arrivals from Canada, which are in general about ten pounds heavier than the wolves that came in the spring of 1995, seem so much more bold, agitated. Some have wondered whether in hindsight it was a mistake to toss an extra wolf into the Nez Perce site, which is the smallest of the Yellowstone acclimation pens. Others have pondered whether this behavior has anything to do with that pen being fairly close to a snowmobile route; is it possible that wolves connect the noises and smells of snowmobiles to the trappers who routinely hunted them in Canada? And yet both these theories fall flat in explaining similar behavior in the Blacktail wolves, who are after all living in thoroughly uncrowded conditions, far from the whine and stink of any snow machines. Furthermore, some of these animals showed aggressive tendencies long before they ever set foot in an acclimation pen, during the initial capture and transport phase. When it's all said and done, this may be just one more example of how all wolves are not alike; packs, as well as individual animals, show extraordinary variations in personality.

One of the more exciting things about the Nez Perce wolves is that up in Canada all were observed feeding on bison. While bison are generally rare in British Columbia, there are some twelve to fifteen hundred free-ranging animals near the latest wolf capture sites at Fort St. John, escaped descendants of a once captive herd of about forty-five purchased by an outfitter back the 1960s. It's the hope of biologists that the Nez Perce wolves weren't just feeding on the carcasses of those bison, the way some of the free-ranging wolves in Yellowstone have done, but were actually *taking* them. Adding bison to the menu at Yellowstone, after all, would greatly expand the prey base. (All the talk of bison hunters, by the way, is spawning yet another notion about why these wolves may be showing more forcefulness: Is it possible that wolves who routinely kill that kind of prey—if these animals are in fact bison hunters—might be genetically predisposed to being more aggressive?)

* * * * *

Not long after Chad McKittrick hit rock bottom back in mid August, running around waving guns and playing outlaw cop and scaring the hell out of his neighbors, there came a generous offer, a helping hand from a concerned family member—a cousin of Chad's named Mike Murphy, who ranches in the wonderful middle of nowhere along the south Musselshell, past where the pavement ends and some forty miles from the nearest bar. Listen, Murphy told Chad, if you think you can stay off drugs and alcohol, get your affairs in order, pack your bags, come up and work for me on the ranch.

In a way it was as close to Chad's old dream as he'd ever gotten, the one he talked of every now and then, about going off somewhere to live a life something like that of a mountain man—be self-sufficient, take his horses and his rifle into the wilds and not look back. The lonely, sprawling country of Mike Murphy's ranch may be starting to nurse Chad out of that nightmare summer. It's been a quiet zone, coaxing him into getting untangled not only from the chemical monkeys hanging off his back, but also from those two-bit pariahs of the anti-wolf movement who'd been such willing sponsors of his demise.

Murphy says as much today, February 26th, speaking on Chad's behalf in a federal courtroom in Billings, Montana, where Chad is about to be sentenced for the killing of wolf number Ten. "I think

166

this is the first time in twenty years Chad's been sober," Murphy tells the judge. "Now maybe he can see the big picture of things. The rednecks in Red Lodge made him out to be the hero. If he wasn't in that setting, I think he'd look at it like he does now, that it was a big mistake." Chad, dressed in jeans and a sport coat, looks on without emotion, staring at his cousin across a chalk-colored cowboy hat turned upside down in front of him on the defense table.

It's not that Chad wouldn't have pulled the trigger on that animal on any given day, especially if he thought it was some kind of varmint; I question whether there's enough rehabilitation anywhere in the world to change that habit, especially when you live your life neck deep in a culture of men who still get off on doing the same thing. But as for regret, well I did see strong hints of that in Chad long ago. And yet today all such arguments on his behalf prove too little, too late. "This was no mistake," Judge Anderson says matter of factly. "No accident. It was an intentional thrill-seeking act in direct violation of the law." The judge goes on to recount how Chad did everything he could to conceal his participation, to hide his crime. "Your post-event conduct established quite a different attitude than remorse. In fact you boasted of having done this act afterward as late as July 4th. This is not acceptance of responsibility. This is the mentality of someone who was willing to kill the animal for thrills, perhaps notoriety. To come in here this morning and tell me (you) accept responsibility flies in the face of the facts." The hens of summer have come home to roost.

"All I can say is I apologize for this," Chad tells the judge. "Sorry for all the trouble."

And with that Anderson sentences Chad to six months incarceration, suggesting that the first half be served at the Yellowstone County jail. Then, in what may be among the more ironic twists of punishment in Montana history, one I could almost imagine making even big wolf number Ten smile from his place in the hereafter—the judge recommends the second half of Chad's sentence be served at a special detention center in Billings: a place known as the Alpha House.

Following lock-up Chad will have one year of supervisory release, during which his person, car, and residence will be subject to random drug testing; furthermore, he'll be required to make himself available to whatever substance abuse program his probation officer thinks is appropriate. As for financial restitution, Anderson says that, while not a condition of release, if Chad ever finds himself of financial means, he'll be required to pay back the government $10,000. When the judge asks if he has any questions, Chad looks at his attorney, gives a slow, enormous shrug of his shoulders, offers a soft, surrendering "no." After the hearing I have a chance to visit with him for a minute, just long enough to ask him how things are going up on the Musselshell.

"Lots of snow," he says, sounding tired, but still managing to push out a small smile. "It's going to be a good year."

*   *   *   *   *

The last week of February and one of Bob Crabtree's coyote project volunteers chances to see Rose Creek's wolf number Nine, along with her new partner originally from the Crystal pack, in an eleven-minute-long copulation tie. Only members of the dog family experience this, and it's caused by a bulb at the base of the male's penis swelling and then being secured by the female's vaginal sphincter muscles, quite literally locking the animals together for anywhere from ten to over thirty minutes, leaving them unable to part even at the approach of danger. After the tie is secured, the male wolf rotates himself out of the original canine-style mounting position, placing his legs beside her and then swinging one hind leg over her back, until the two animals are tail to tail; the pair usually lies quietly in that position for the duration of the tie. Only a tiny percentage of courtship attempts actually result in copulation. Dave Mech reports that during field observations of a wolf pack on Isle Royale over three separate breeding seasons, he saw actual copulation occur only four times. Though no one really knows the purpose of such ties, we again almost have to wonder whether the real value is to strengthen the bond between the alpha pair; that may be especially important in wolves like Nine and Eight, mating for the very first time.

With the news of this coupling it occurs to me that, short of the kind of all-consuming attack launched on their kind through the early decades of the twentieth century, perhaps these wolves are here to stay after all, at least in Yellowstone. Their tenacity, their astonishing adaptability in the face of changing circumstances—in short that very thing that has kept all those unseemly myths about them smoldering for centuries—is precisely what will allow them to survive, even thrive. Maybe it really does, as Mike Phillips once told me, come down to a matter of giving them one good chance, and then just getting out of the way.

*　*　*　*　*

The days are swelling toward spring, wrapping the land once again in a muddling mix of snow and cold, sun and warmth and wind. In a few days it'll be one year since the fences were cut and wolves finally walked free in Yellowstone. And in truth it seems things are as settled right now as they've been in all that time. Though they'll soon run back to the Beartooth front, for the moment the Soda Butte group, complete with pup, is back in those yawning meadows and burned-out woods that cradle Slough Creek, right on the park border, near the Silver Tip guest ranch. Seven (originally from Rose Creek) and Two (from Crystal)—the nucleus of what will become the Leopold pack—are hanging tight on the Blacktail Plateau, while Rose Creek, at nine animals the biggest of the packs, is a dozen miles away, often visible, drawn in again and again to an acclimation pen that holds two adults and two yearlings fresh in from Canada. And finally the three remaining members of the Crystal pack, those grand entertainers from that unforgettable summer of 1995, are home again in the valley of the Lamar.

THIRTEEN

From the double window above my desk I look past the leafless ribbon of aspen and cottonwood cradling Rock Creek, southward onto the dark, piney shoulders of Mount Maurice, where a year ago number Nine lay down in a scrape of dirt under a spruce tree and gave birth to eight pups. To the east, out my living room window, is the open flank of a long, flat bench, beyond which in that same season number Ten took his last breath on a treeless, sage-covered hill above the old mining camps of Scotch Coulee, felt the sting of a bullet in his side, collapsed, and died. To the north are the open pastures where the Soda Butte group showed up this past January, a month before calving season, leaving ranchers swearing, their teeth clenched around a fear so old it seems petrified.

This is wolf country now. Wolf country again. And that single fact has stirred more imaginations, kindled more fear and fancy, hatred and thrill than any other single happening along the face of these mountains in decades. My neighbors hold a range of feelings as wide as the prairie sky. Some are enthralled, enchanted by this added measure of wildness in an already wild place; fond of the animal, to be sure, but more than that, gratified to think their back yard is one of only a few places left in the temperate world with the same mix of mammals that roamed here hundreds of years ago. On the other horizon are those for whom this reintroduction is a contemptible act—reckless, unthinking. Another nail in the coffin which when added to things like rampant subdivisions and meat-packing monopolies seems destined to end the rancher's way of life forever. "Americans don't much like the rancher anymore," one cattleman told me recently. "Bringing back the wolf is proof enough of that."

But the overwhelming national support for this reintroduction really shouldn't come as a surprise. For all our environmental neglect, we've had a long, recurring history of wanting to heal our wild places. We'd barely reached the end of the 1600s before people were decrying—mostly on spiritual grounds—what they saw as the wholesale destruction of wildlife in southeast New England. A hundred years later, as a brand new country we struggled mightily to forge a sense of national identity, grasping for a cultural vision to hold up against the overwhelming centuries of art and music and history that was Europe. In the end it was our weave of mountain and forest that we put on a pedestal, calling it proof of our being a chosen people, using it as bedrock for both our patriotism and our religion.

Admittedly, two centuries later things aren't so simple. These days we seem hamstrung by the desire to broaden our concept of what it means to tend nature—pushing hard for the need to think in terms of ecosystems—while at the same time remaining clueless about how to factor people into the equation. Having one foot in the spiritual side of nature without the other being ankle-deep in the muck of daily life—the price of cattle and the cost of rent—can lead to folly. Too often we think that as long as we truly love that sweeping view outside our picture windows, as long as we keep writing checks to bring back the wolves or stop the clear cuts, somehow that will be enough.

The more bizarre notions of the anti-wolf movement—that wolves are little more than the devil's messengers, determined to steal children and nab every cow in sight—will eventually crumble. And slowly but surely, as the years pass it'll become clear to ranchers that this is not the same world it was a hundred years ago, when game populations had been so thoroughly ravaged by humans that predators of all kinds were pushed into lunching on domestic livestock. Perhaps more uncertain are the kinds of attitudes that will evolve in those who now claim to be in favor of wolves. When the time comes for controlling wolves—and that time *will* come—will supporters decide such management isn't okay after all? It's a scary thought. If those who support wolves turn their backs on the real and reasonable concerns of ranchers, they'll not only create a backlash that makes the illegal killing of wolves going on now look like child's play, but strike a death knell for the future of holistic wildlife management for years to come.

If somehow we manage to make it, if ranchers can let go of fairy tales and wolf proponents can more fully squeeze people into their sense of place, then maybe one day we'll have something few ever counted on when wolves came home to Yellowstone: the beginning of a new conservation—an ethic that works both in the heart and on the ground.

* * * * *

Tonight I lie in my bed and think of them. Mostly the seventeen wolves just released, wondering what might be going through their heads as they make their way out to the wild, ragged edges of this new world. It's hard for me not to marvel now at lives so devoted to group, bonded in ways that seem both familiar and unfathomable—linked by fantastical threads that pull them through the ebb and flow of the hunt, nudge them into playfulness, lend them the urge to all stop on some windswept ridge and unleash round after round of howling. And yet even with that they maintain a striking individuality: confident or cowering; playful or serious; some that will live all their days retiring and shy, others that will die full of fire. And all of them, it seems, destined to leave human theories about who they are and what they will do riddled with exceptions.

All I can say for sure is that tonight they run. Twists of shadow in the moonlight of early spring, coursing up the willow bottoms and through the lodgepole forests—buoyed by those massive paws, rising and falling like whispers against the snow.

© Scott Prather

About the Author

Gary Ferguson has been a free-lance writer for fifteen years. His science and nature articles have appeared in more than 100 national magazines, including *Outside*, *Big Sky Journal*, *Sierra*, *Travel-Holiday*, and *Modern Maturity*.

Gary is the author of eight books on nature, including the upcoming *Spirits of the Wild*, a collection of nature tales from around the world, published by Clarkson Potter; *Walking Down the Wild*, from HarperCollins West; and the acclaimed *Walks of* natural/cultural series from Fulcrum Publishing. His 1990 coffee table book, *Montana National Forests*, published by Falcon Press, received the National Association for Interpretation Award for Excellence in Communication.

Before beginning his writing career, Gary spent four years as an interpretive naturalist in the Sawtooth Mountains of Idaho. He makes his home in Red Lodge, Montana.

*　*　*　*　*